SHADOWS AT WORK

HARNESS YOUR DARK SIDE AND UNLOCK YOUR LEADERSHIP POTENTIAL

STEVEN D'SOUZA

PRAISE FOR *SHADOWS AT WORK*

"Steven D'Souza extends a bold and necessary invitation to step out of the binaries of light and dark and into the richer, more nuanced terrain of what makes us human. This book will keep you thinking long after you've turned the final page."
Daniel H. Pink, #1 *New York Times* bestselling author of *The Power of Regret, Drive* and *When*

"*Shadows at Work* is an essential read for leaders, teams and organisations ready to confront the unseen forces shaping workplace culture. With a rare blend of depth and accessibility, D'Souza takes us on a journey through the hidden dynamics that influence behaviour, decisions and relationships at work. Rather than ignoring or suppressing these 'shadows,' he encourages us to engage with them, revealing how they can be transformed into sources of growth, creativity and connection. This book challenges the conventional wisdom of leadership and organisational culture, offering fresh insights into what it truly means to build workplaces that are not just productive, but also human. If you're serious about leading with awareness and authenticity, *Shadows at Work* belongs on your shelf."
Dr. Marshall Goldsmith, *Thinkers50* #1 Executive Coach and *New York Times* bestselling author of *The Earned Life, Triggers* and *What Got You Here Won't Get You There*

"Leadership is too easily and exclusively associated with glory and success. There is much more to being a leader. True leadership requires groundedness, humility, realism and a genuine appreciation of the highs and lows which are part of all lives – and all organisations. Steven D'Souza has written a thought-provoking and wide-ranging guide to the shadows of leadership. By understanding the shadows we can appreciate the light."
Stuart Crainer & **Des Dearlove**, Founders, Thinkers50

"In *Shadows at Work*, Steven D'Souza offers a profound and dynamic framework for leaders and managers to understand and harness the often-overlooked 'dark side' within themselves. By exploring shadows through four interconnected lenses – cultural, physiological, psychological and spiritual – D'Souza empowers readers to unlock their full potential, making this book an indispensable guide in navigating the complexities of leadership, particularly in an age dominated by AI."
Santiago Iniguez, President, IE University

"An enlightened and essential call to action for leaders to confront their hidden selves to transform their organisations from the inside out."
David Burkus, Author of *Best Team Ever*

"I have had the privilege of knowing Steven D'Souza for over 20 years, and his thoughtfulness, wisdom and ability to challenge conventional thinking have always stood out. *Shadows at Work* is a timely and profound exploration of the hidden dynamics that shape our personal and professional lives. In this book, Steven brings his unique perspective to illuminate the concept of the Shadow in leadership – a topic that is often overlooked but is critically important. This concise yet impactful guide invites leaders and managers to embark on a journey of self-awareness and integration, offering insights that are both practical and transformative. Steven's ability to weave together psychological, cultural and spiritual dimensions ensures that it will resonate with a wide audience, inspiring them to embrace the complexity of leadership with courage and compassion. I highly recommend this book to anyone who seeks to grow as a leader and create meaningful change in their organisation and beyond."
Dr. Patrick Clarke, OBE, Director of Network Operations, UK Power Networks

"Having known Steven for more than 35 years, his insights are always interesting and well-thought-out. Building on the transformative themes of his earlier works, this book offers a compelling exploration of the unseen and darker forces that shape leadership. With his trademark blend of wisdom and practicality, Steven challenges readers to confront their shadows, fostering authenticity and growth. A must-read for anyone seeking to lead with courage and depth, embracing the good in their dark side."
Mark Wright, COO, Impactable Investment Group

"Midlife presents us with both the opportunity and the psychological maturity to fully confront our Shadows. We become aware of the paths not taken and the dreams we have deferred. *Shadows at Work* by Steven D'Souza is a clarion call to reflect now on what truly matters to us. By honouring our Shadows we uncover their treasures and gifts that will enrich the remainder of our lives."
Chip Conley, Co-founder, Modern Elder Academy, author of *Wisdom@Work*

"The literature on leadership development is replete with artificial dichotomies. *Shadows at Work* shows us that a more complex and nuanced approach is required to experience the profound impact and effectiveness that leaders can have on everyone around them, business and society when they are equipped to intentionally embrace both their dark and light sides. D'Souza presents a way to do just that. Whether you're an executive or a first-time leader, this is the book you need to explore and embrace your dark side – to access your whole self and benefit from greater clarity, creativity and fulfilling connections within yourself and the world around you, to create a better future."
Anushia Reddy, Psychologist, Talent Development

"With remarkable insight and compassion, this book illuminates the full spectrum of human experience in leadership. By exploring both light and shadow, the author helps us understand not just how to lead, but what it truly means to be human in our complex organisational lives."
Adam Taffler, Founder, Togetherness

"This book is exceptionally rich and fruitful. Steven is a master storyteller and manages to take us to deep and challenging places, and at the same time reveals how integration of dark and light is vital to living the good life. What this book does beautifully is weave together individual experience with societal influences, bringing new insights into how facing into the shadow can help light up our souls. I highly recommend this book for both personal insights, and also for those working in organisations such as HR and OD functions, as it helps us understand the challenges we face and offers ways to help transcend these."
Simon Western, CEO and founder, The Eco-Leadership Institute

"In this very personal examination, Steven sheds light on the dark side of our work lives – everything that remains unsaid and suppressed when we perform as our consistent, productive selves – and shows us that we can only humanise business if we accept all of life into it, including fear, pain, loss and grief. A beautifully candid, humane book."
Tim Lebrecht, Co-founder, House of Beautiful Business

"Steven D'Souza is an inspiration and his new book is both an efficient and lyrical treasure trove for mining both the dark and the light in our modern world."
Jamie Catto, Author, musician, film director and founding member, Faithless and 1 Giant Leap

"This is a deeply thoughtful, profound and useful book, yet very easy to read. The author is a rare combination of a widely-read business consultant with coaching experience who thinks about the big questions of life. The structure of the book encourages the reader to ponder some of the most important questions of all ... and how to answer them. A masterpiece!"
Adrian Furnham, Professor of Psychology, Birkbeck, University of London

"Steven D'Souza's new book is a breath of fresh air that invites us to embrace the shadow not just as a place of barriers and derailers that must be managed, but as the very source of our creativity and humanity. A must-read for leaders committed to developing themselves and others to achieve their full potential."
Jennifer Petriglieri, Associate Professor, INSEAD

"This brilliant and fascinating book is a compelling read. D'Souza's exploration of our Shadow self not only helps the reader better understand themselves and their behaviour in a range of situations, it is also an essential guide to how we can develop stronger connections and deeper, more empathic relationships with our colleagues and team members as a result of that understanding."
Andy Lopata, Speaker, podcast host, author of *The Financial Times Guide to Mentoring*

"Once again, Steven D'Souza masterfully holds up a mirror to help us see those aspects of ourselves that we cannot see, or perhaps don't want to. He conveys powerful lessons with a wonderful lightness that makes the book accessible to a wide audience. One of the insights that can make an immediate impact in business is how low self-perceptions can manifest in inhibited performance or even self-sabotage, due to fear of failure or, indeed, fear of success. Shining the light of awareness on these 'shadows' can transfer energy from negative rumination to positive actions."
Gulamabbas Lakha, CEO, Providential Capital LLP

"*Shadows at Work* is all about what we hide from ourselves, how we can make friends with it, and all the good stuff that will follow. The author generously shares with us a treasure of knowledge (beautifully weaving in thoughts of so many researchers and writers), along with a very gentle vibe of unforced curiosity and empathetic optimism. I find the book to be a most alluring invitation to change."
Itay Talgam, Conductor, author of *The Ignorant Maestro*

"In this book, Steven D'Souza has provided a comprehensive introduction to the Shadow that is both accessible and provocative. He goes far beyond a Jungian frame of reference to provide a rich banquet of concepts and inspirations. Drawing on a wide range of ideas, he brings the Shadow to life and illustrates its significance as a timeless archetype. This book leaves the reader with a lot to think about and a lot more to explore."
Laurence Barrett, Author of *A Jungian Approach to Coaching*

"Our current busyness obsession pulls our attention to the predictable and controllable, sabotaging our capacity to inquire and engage with vital complex, often scary questions. Ignoring the unsaid and the unheard is an evasion of responsibility. In *Shadows at Work*, D'Souza marks out a way for leaders to attend to and mine the fundamental insights and gifts that lurk in the Shadows."
Megan Reitz, Author of *Speak Out, Listen Up*, Associate Fellow, Saïd Business School, Oxford University

"It's said the gold is in the dark. But who's brave enough to venture in alone? This book makes a trusted companion."
Michael Bungay Stanier, Author of *The Coaching Habit*

"Steven D'Souza's *Shadows at Work* offers a thoughtful exploration of the hidden aspects of our professional lives. Steven's deep insights into the interplay of light and shadow within us provide a compelling guide to embracing and integrating our darker sides. His interdisciplinary approach, weaving together psychology, philosophy and real-world examples offers practical strategies for personal and organisational growth. This book is particularly valuable for talent leaders and leadership developers, emphasising the importance of recognising and addressing potential derailers. I have found Steven's work both enlightening and empowering, and have successfully applied his principles in my own professional environment. It is an essential read for anyone looking to unlock their full potential and lead with authenticity and empathy."
Dr. Nina Kreyer, Head Learning and Development,
LGT Private Banking

"*Shadows at Work* is one of those rare books that makes you stop, reflect and see yourself, and the world, differently. Steven takes a concept we often shy away from, our Shadows, and shows how embracing them can make us better leaders, colleagues and humans. Thought-provoking, nuanced and practical, this book challenges the simplistic narratives of 'good' and 'bad' leadership, and instead offers a richer, more honest way to grow. A compelling read for anyone serious about self-awareness and real impact."
Shakil Nathoo, Partner, Leader in Strategic Operations,
Kearney

"*Shadows at Work* offers a profound examination of how our shadows shape our view of the world and those within it, through the lenses of culture, physiology, psychology and spirituality. It is an invitation to stop trying to change who we are, but rather accept our dark side – our shadows – to harness our hidden depths and potential. Steven brilliantly illuminates how, through 'shadow work' and being 'present within the darkness,' we can learn to transcend our blind spots. How to face up to our inner critic, as we project and label others with the shadows we fear to face in ourselves. How to think differently about the safe spaces we create in organisations, when we risk shielding their people from experiences of self-discovery. And how leaders, as they ascend their organisation, need to develop not just a new role, but a new sense of identity. *Shadows at Work* is a wake-up call for any leader who wishes to turn toward what we have been conditioned to avoid. The book brilliantly exposes how 'shadow rules' – those hidden dynamics that manifest our organisations' cultural norms and subtle societal pressures – shape our lives. To do so, Steven draws on a wonderfully eclectic set of real-life examples to bring shadow work to life, most poignantly his own personal journey. Amidst increasing socio-political polarisation, *Shadows at Work* encourages us to hold the space for multiple truths; to see the light in the darkness. This is an important book for our times, one that reveals deep truths about what it means to be human."
James Woodcock, Partner, Korn Ferry, author of *Ego Flip*

"Steven's book is not only provocative but really timely as we struggle through late-stage capitalism to figure out the next evolution of organising humans for the progression of our civilisation. At Blue Fire AI, we constantly identify global companies that are at risk of collapse. It is shocking how often most of these situations are a result of non-integrated shadows of management, shareholders or employees expressing unfettered drives cloaked with 'good' intentions. This is an important piece of work with relatable anecdotes to help the reader progress on their journey to harnessing their shadows, to become a more complete and well-formed version of themself. Everything that is new and progressive comes from our collective shadows that have been rejected by society, norms, traditions and laws."
Samir Rath, CEO, Co-founder, Blue Fire AI

"Through a thoughtful exploration of cultural, physiological, psychological and spiritual dimensions, *Shadows at Work* provides an insightful framework to understand how shadows are formed and expressed within ourselves and our organisations. As an accessible and practical guide, this book offers valuable insights for HR professionals and those involved in organisational transformation, linking personal shadows to broader patterns of collective behaviour. For leaders, the book serves as an invitation to a profound personal journey – where light, as the essence of human flourishing, finds its counterpoint in shadow – encouraging us to embrace their dialectical dance to uncover a deeper, more authentic wisdom and step into our fullest potential."
Otti Vogt, Founder, Global Society for Good Leadership, Former Chief Transformation Officer, ING

"It's sincerely difficult to do Steven's body of writing in *Shadows at Work* justice in a short endorsement, yet it is needed. Battered by a crazy modern world, this book is your survival guide. You can reserve judgement on this being hyperbole all you like. This book is too important to overlook. It's beyond a superbly crafted tome; it's a call to the depths of our very souls, which may make it difficult for people to choose this book. But please, do choose it. Or, risk living and working in a darker form of self than you deserve."
Perry Timms, Founder and Chief Energy Officer, People and Transformational HR, 2022's *HR* Most Influential Thinker

"*Shadows at Work* is not a self-improvement manual. It acknowledges the human character comprises both light and shadow aspects. It is a guide to explore our shadow side, the side that often lurks hidden in the subconscious. Steven D'Souza references his personal experiences, psychology, art, literature and film to make his points, and to probe the reader to dig deeper about what makes one tick and develop conscious and healthy relationships with our shadows. The reflections and questions at the end of each chapter spurred me to explore my experiences in more detail and get insights into my own journey. *Shadows at Work* is an opportunity to develop a conscious and healthy relationship with our shadow, and harvest this to be a better leader."
Michael Frawley, Chief Risk Officer

Published by
LID Publishing
An imprint of LID Business Media Ltd.
LABS House, 15–19 Bloomsbury Way,
London, WC1A 2TH, UK

info@lidpublishing.com
www.lidpublishing.com

A member of:

BPR ✦
businesspublishersroundtable.com

ISBN: 978-1-917391-41-2
ISBN: 978-1-917391-42-9 (ebook)

Cover design: Henry Steadman
Page design: Caroline Li
Illustrations: Jess May Palmer

SHADOWS AT WORK

HARNESS YOUR DARK SIDE AND UNLOCK YOUR LEADERSHIP POTENTIAL

STEVEN D'SOUZA

LID

MADRID | MEXICO CITY | LONDON
BUENOS AIRES | BOGOTA | SHANGHAI

For Danielle, Ethan and Lucas.
May you always be loved for all that you are.

If only it were all so simple!
If only there were evil people
somewhere insidiously committing
evil deeds, and it were necessary
only to separate them from the
rest of us and destroy them. But
the line dividing good and evil
cuts through the heart of every
human being. And who is willing to
destroy a piece of his own heart?

Alexander Solzhenitsyn
The Gulag Archipelago, Volume 1

A leader is someone with the power to project either shadow or light onto some part of the world and onto the lives of the people who dwell there. A leader shapes the ethos in which others must live, an ethos as light-filled as heaven or as shadowy as hell. A good leader is intensely aware of the interplay of inner shadow and light, lest the act of leadership do more harm than good.

Parker J. Palmer
Let Your Life Speak

CONTENTS

FOREWORD

When we think about human potential, we often gravitate toward ideals like strength, virtue and light. Yet, as psychologists, leaders and students of human behaviour, we know that the complete picture of human potential resides not just in the bright and polished, but also in the murky depths of our psyche, including those character traits and dispositions that cast a shadow over our bright side, effectively limiting or handicapping our potential.

Indeed, throughout history, eminent philosophers and writers have often been captivated by the concept of the Shadow aspects of human nature, exploring the hidden, repressed or morally ambiguous elements of individual character and personality.

This fascination can be traced back to ancient myths and tragedies such as the works of Sophocles, whose play *Oedipus Rex* delved into fate, guilt and the unconscious forces shaping human behaviour. In the 19th century, Romantic and Gothic literature embraced the shadow self, with Mary Shelley's *Frankenstein* examining hubris and the monstrous consequences of unchecked ambition.

Likewise, philosophers like Friedrich Nietzsche explored themes of inner conflict and the will to power, emphasising the importance of confronting one's darker instincts to achieve self-actualisation. The early 20th century saw Carl Jung formalise the concept of the Shadow in psychology, positing it as a crucial part of the unconscious mind containing repressed desires and fears. Writers such as Fyodor Dostoevsky and Franz Kafka examined moral ambiguity and existential despair as their characters wrestled with guilt, alienation and societal pressures.

In modern literature and pop culture, figures like Joseph Conrad in *Heart of Darkness* and George Orwell in *1984* interrogated the Shadow not just within individuals, but in institutions and ideologies, exploring how power and corruption manifest in dark and dehumanising ways.

Collectively, these thinkers and creators illuminate the necessity of engaging with the Shadow to understand the complexities of human nature and the potential for growth, redemption or destruction inherent within us all. Their work underscores that the exploration of the dark side is not merely an indulgence in negativity but a profound inquiry into what it means to be human.

Steven D'Souza's book, *Shadows at Work: Harness Your Dark Side and Unlock Your Full Potential*, dares to navigate that complexity. It challenges us to recognise, embrace and integrate the hidden aspects of ourselves that conventional wisdom often urges us to suppress. It is a manifesto for becoming whole, not just as individuals but as members of organisations and society.

As someone who has spent years exploring the psychological traits that differentiate great leaders from the rest, I have learned that success and authenticity often hinge on paradoxes. Those who lead effectively are not necessarily the most talented, but rather those capable of self-awareness, including an understanding of their Shadow self and how to tame or inhibit the counterproductive side of their personality. They are not defined by their perfections but by their ability to learn from imperfections, containing their inner demons instead of being possessed or controlled by them. The premise of this book, therefore, is profoundly resonant: our Shadows are not obstacles to overcome but resources to tap into. They are the untamed forces that, when recognised and understood, can propel us toward innovation, empathy and growth.

Throughout history, the metaphor of light versus darkness has shaped how we perceive ourselves and others. It's easy to relegate 'darkness' to the realm of negativity, weakness or even evil, yet these constructs are often societal projections that obscure the more nuanced reality. The Shadow, as articulated by Jung, is not merely the repository of what we reject about ourselves but also the container of unrealised strengths, creativity and potential. If ignored, it may manifest destructively, but if engaged with courage and compassion, it can become a source of profound transformation.

Shadows at Work builds on this foundational idea with refreshing clarity and practical relevance. It translates abstract psychological concepts into tangible insights applicable to the modern workplace. In doing so, it transcends the dichotomy of self-help and leadership theory. This is not a manual for quick fixes or surface-level improvements. Instead, it's a guide for leaders, employees and anyone willing to embark on a journey of self-discovery to confront their vulnerabilities, biases and blind spots. The book recognises that, in a world that prizes productivity and perfection, allowing ourselves to wrestle with our Shadows can feel counterintuitive. Yet, as the author shows, this is precisely the work that matters most.

One of the book's key strengths lies in its interdisciplinary approach. By weaving together insights from psychology, philosophy, literature and real-world examples, the author paints a rich and textured picture of how Shadows operate within us and within organisations. This is crucial because the workplace is often where our Shadows are most likely to emerge. Whether through hierarchical structures, unspoken norms or interpersonal dynamics, our workplaces serve as magnifying glasses for the parts of ourselves we'd rather not see. The book challenges us to face these truths and offers strategies to do so constructively.

Importantly, this is not just a book about individual growth; it's also about systemic change. By exploring concepts like projection, defence mechanisms and collective Shadows, it highlights how the dynamics of power, culture and leadership influence the environments we create. Leaders, in particular, bear a heavy responsibility. Their Shadows, when unchecked, can be detrimental to entire organisations. Conversely, leaders who courageously confront their darker sides not only inspire trust but also cultivate cultures of openness and resilience. In this way, *Shadows at Work* is as much a call to action for organisational reform as it is for personal transformation.

Importantly, D'Souza's vulnerability in sharing his own journey lends authenticity to the book's insights. By recounting moments of conflict, self-doubt and growth, he reminds us that 'shadow work' is deeply human. It is not about achieving perfection but about striving for balance and integration. This message is particularly urgent in our polarised world, where the refusal to acknowledge complexity often fuels division and misunderstanding.

In reading this book, you will be invited to reflect on your own Shadows, but also to reimagine what's possible for the teams, organisations and communities you are part of. You will be challenged to question assumptions, embrace contradictions and, ultimately, to lead with greater authenticity and empathy. These are not easy tasks, but they are necessary ones. If the book teaches us anything, it's that by welcoming the Shadows, we don't lose ourselves. We become more fully who we are.

As you turn these pages, prepare to step into a space that is at once challenging and liberating, unsettling and enlightening. Embrace the Shadows, and you will find the light within them.

Tomas Chamorro-Premuzic, PhD
Professor of Business Psychology at Columbia and University College London, Chief Innovation Officer at ManpowerGroup

you
ed a
rre-
im-
Ju

INTRODUCTION

Only it builds up, doesn't it?
It doesn't just disappear. And
one day you start prodding at
what you've suppressed. And
it's a mass of black rot, and it's
endless, horrifying, and you
can't look away.

R. F. Kuang
Babel

We find beauty not in the thing itself but in the patterns of shadows, the light and darkness, that one thing against another creates.

Jun'ichirō Tanizaki
In Praise of Shadows

The heavy door slammed shut. As Michael Tippett lay down on the cell's hard bed, thin strips of light faded to darkness. It was a relief to know that this was his last night of a three-month internment in London's infamous Wormwood Scrubs Prison. Finally, he could return to the work that only he was meant to do.

Until his death in 1998 at the age of 93, Sir Michael Tippett was considered one of Britain's leading composers. Yet his energetic, off-beat music is rarely heard in concert halls or in mainstream playlists today. Music was the vehicle through which he reflected on ideas and explored the thornier issues relating to humanity and society, including race, class, sexism, war and social justice; issues as relevant now as they were then.

Shortly before his incarceration, and just two days after the outbreak of the Second World War, Tippett composed *A Child of Our Time*. This piece was inspired by the story of a Polish Jewish refugee living in Paris in 1938 who responded to the news that his parents had been deported from Germany by shooting a Nazi diplomat. The assassination was used as the excuse for the monstrous violence of *Kristallnacht* (the Night of Broken Glass).

The music is based on five African American spirituals. Tippett wanted to tap into the way these religious folk songs convey a deep understanding of human suffering, while also directing attention beyond the nascent conflict in Europe. He believed it was everyone's responsibility to care for the marginalised, for *the other*, no matter their race, creed or gender.

A Child of Our Time has a stark opening: "The world turns on its dark side," the chorus intones. "It is winter." Terror reigns. The violence is graphic. There are sung exhortations to curse and kill.

> *Burn down their houses!*
> *Beat in their heads!*
> *Break them in pieces on the wheel!*

The terrible brutality of *A Child of Our Time* resonates today, with the global and local conflicts we still see, decades after its composition. Yet, despite the great darkness, there remains hope for humanity. Light will return and there will be an opportunity for renewal.

I would know my shadow and my light, so shall I at last be whole.
Then courage, brother, dare the grave passage.
Here is no final grieving, but an abiding hope.
The moving waters renew the earth. It is spring.

The motif of integrating both the light and dark is crucial for the arrival of the new spring. For Tippett, these are opposites that humanity needs to engage with and unify. Only by working actively across the full spectrum can we hope to find wholeness, individually and collectively.

When Tippett emerged from his prison cell, he felt vindicated that declining the forced manual labour imposed on him as a conscientious objector to the war was the right thing to have done. Although he had spent time teaching music to the underprivileged, running a summer camp near mining towns and starting an orchestra for unemployed musicians, Tippett had come to realise that the world needed less ideals-driven political activism and more psychological balance. Music was how he would achieve this. Through it, he questioned the world we live in and how we behave in it.

Tippett's insights have as much relevance today as they did when he composed and wrote the libretto for *A Child of Our Time*. To understand ourselves, to complete ourselves, to better ourselves, we need to be as familiar with the Shadows as with the light. This is critical for us personally, but also for our work, our organisations, our leadership and our increasingly polarised society. Without it, we risk recreating the violence of Tippett's chorus in perpetuity.

A PERSONAL JOURNEY

Every book reveals something of the life of the author, and *Shadows At Work* is no exception. I grew up in a strongly Catholic family in a small town in England, where ideas of good and bad, light and dark, were prescribed and embedded. Doing the right thing was rewarded, while doing the opposite was treated as a moral transgression, causing guilt, shame and a desire to be and do better.

The culture I grew up in seemed to present a binary choice: you were either the hero or the villain, Superman or Lex Luthor, the playful Jerry or the conniving Tom. There were no shades of grey or complexity. Of course, I failed to live up to these ideals, even if they ultimately were meant to lead to happiness. Over time, though, I became more interested in what was driving me to appear perfect and the cost I paid for it. Admitting to secrecy, lies, guilt and shame during confession would result in temporary respite and new resolve before the cycle would begin again.

This carried over into the start of my adult life, where I still aspired to the perfect embodiment of ideals and values. Initially, I trained as a priest for two years, but found that label and the constraints that came with it too oppressive, preventing me from becoming a whole person. I was enjoying comforts that did not align with my understanding of a life of service and seemed at odds with my involvement in a community dedicated to poverty. The signs had been there even before I joined the seminary, reflected in a psychologist's report when I was nineteen:

> *Contrasts and dichotomies feature in Steven's thinking, between light and dark, heaven and hell, ecstasy and desolation. I think it may be difficult for him to work with loss, grief and sadness and to find holiness in pain or a sense of emptiness, as well as in adoration.*

The other contrast with which he is struggling is that between a sense of loneliness, reflection, quietness, solitude and peacefulness, on the one hand, and risk, adventure, growth and possibilities of relationship on the other. This is not really a dichotomy, since the two are not mutually exclusive. What is difficult is finding a means of holding them together.

At the time, my view of the world was fundamentally altered when I read the psychotherapist Sheldon Kopp's book, *If You Meet Buddha on the Road, Kill Him!* I realised that I needed to slay my proverbial sacred cows and challenge my conceptual Buddhas, to move away from untested ideals and step closer to reality. I decided to leave the seminary and study at university instead.

Over 30 years later, my career has seen me leading in organisations as well as consulting to dozens more. I have experienced different work environments in a variety of countries and industries. Certainly, there are some of the latter – investment banking and the tobacco industry – that my childhood self would have thought morally questionable. So, like Anakin Skywalker, have I been tempted by the Dark Side? Or have I found a more nuanced and balanced view of the world, where I can work in challenging industries and help them transition their businesses and practices?

I remember dining with a colleague before accepting the tobacco job, sharing my internal conflict with her. Should I work for a company that manufactured harmful products even if my role was intended to hasten its transformation? Was I deceiving myself, being wilfully blind, simply following the money? Rather than criticise, condemn or physically recoil from me as others had done, she opted to tell me a story.

Rumi, the Sufi mystic, was a pupil of the Persian poet and spiritual instructor Shams. One day, Shams asked him to fetch a bottle of wine from the local town. Horrified, Rumi objected. "I cannot do this. I'm a holy man. What will people think of me?" Nevertheless, Rumi obeyed, closely following Shams's instructions. He purchased the wine and carried it in full view of the onlooking villagers. When he reached his teacher, Shams took the bottle, held it high and poured its contents on the floor.

Clearly, this short but powerful story was not about the wine. My friend was telling me that to do our work, sometimes the hardest thing we must do is stop caring about what others think of us or about how we judge ourselves.

This book is not an argument for moral relativism, but it does advocate increased appreciation for complexity, as well as holding in check our tendency to rush to judge others. Some of the most engaged organisations I have worked with have been perceived by others as pariah companies, yet some of the most toxic have included charities. The irony is not lost on me.

I strongly believe that we need to go beyond the simplistic differentiation between 'heroic' and 'bad' leaders. We must recognise that such labels fail to capture the complexity of what it means to be human. Reductionism is dangerous, blinding us to what is in ourselves and others. When we recognise and *own* our foibles and weaknesses, when we can understand, embrace and meet our darkest traits with compassion, we are more likely to extend understanding to others instead of passing judgement.

A LEADERSHIP CHALLENGE

Treating other people with empathy, care and understanding, regardless of their position, status, beliefs, values or perspectives, is vital to effective leadership. But I have learned during my career that these qualities are rarely as evident as they should be, because our dominant leadership paradigm tends to be authoritarian, controlling and frequently narcissistic. This is especially true at the very top of corporate hierarchies. This is not to suggest that all leaders act in this way, but it does highlight the fact that the exceptions are more notable for their rarity.

Sadly, too many leaders lack awareness of the harm done by their own behaviours, biases and actions. They do not see how what is repressed in themselves infects other people. Rather than nurturing the development of those they lead, they end up inhibiting and suppressing their latent skills and capabilities, preventing the full expression of their personalities.

But it is not my purpose here to denigrate business or capitalism or leadership. Rather, I want to emphasise how everything has a Shadow side that needs to be acknowledged and engaged. As we shall see, this extends to each of us, as individuals, as teams, as communities and as organisations. We cannot live without our Shadows, which are composed of the unconscious parts of ourselves that we do not identify with, often containing qualities we would rather not acknowledge, including gifts we have not yet expressed.

Just as we carry inside us both the light and the dark that Tippett alludes to, so do our institutions and those who lead them. For many of us, in fact, work is something that provides meaning in our lives. It can be a source of purpose and satisfaction, where we utilise our knowledge and skills to give and receive value.

But it also can be a cause of frustration, fear, worry, heartache, anger and thwarted personal and professional development.

Business is one of our many social systems. It is entirely relational. It depends on interaction between people, on knowledge sharing, influence, encouragement, feedback, motivation, compromise and so many other nuanced exchanges. The way leaders behave and respond, therefore, has an enormous impact on the people they work with. The smallest thing, often done or said without thinking, can have an adverse effect. Whether intentionally or not, leaders cast a long shadow over their organisations' culture.

In *Steps to an Ecology of Mind,* the anthropologist Gregory Bateson referred to systemic wisdom, which is the ability to see and work with whole systems rather than isolated parts. This capacity to understand context, to sense relationships, to work with complexity, represents a form of intelligence that we have often devalued in favour of more linear, analytical thinking. Integrating this systemic wisdom is central to navigating and transforming the Shadow systems that shape our lives as individuals and organisations.

But the lack of systemic awareness becomes evident as issues evolve into structural patterns. The unreflective leader's desires and preferences are enshrined in policy and process, shaping their organisation's culture. Those who conform are celebrated and rewarded. But where people can find no cultural alignment, their own desires and preferences must be suppressed. They begin to feel under-appreciated, become disengaged or stuck, or choose to quietly quit. This can erode trust and impact performance. It can also result in transgressive behaviour when what has been suppressed suddenly bubbles to the surface in angry outbursts, demonstrations of jealousy and moments of incivility.

Of course, these patterns and behaviours are not confined to the workplace. They play out in all aspects of our lives. In families, in personal relationships, in one-to-one interactions, in team dynamics, in organisational culture, in politics, in international affairs. But it is in the workplace that we spend a significant proportion of our adult lives, and it is there that our Shadow personalities often can be activated.

TWO TALES

Consider the case of Howard Beale. In the Oscar-winning movie *Network*, television news anchor Beale (Peter Finch) has been a compliant company man for many years, patiently towing the party line. His imminent redundancy because of low ratings triggers something in him, releasing a wellspring of pent-up emotions and suicidal tendencies. All that has been repressed by corporate policy, authoritarian leadership and broadcasting standards erupts in an outpouring of anger and rage. "I'm mad as hell," he yells, "and I'm not going to take this anymore."

Despite the attempts of authority figures in the TV network to bully, coerce and manipulate Beale, over the course of his live broadcasts he begins to influence others with his message. What once was personal has now become collective. A ratings spike leads to the exploitation of Beale's new-found popularity by the ambitious head of programming Diana Christensen (Faye Dunaway). But it also mobilises forces of resistance by those who wish to protect the status quo, including a chilling intervention by the network's holding company chairman, Arthur Jensen (Ned Beatty), who hopes to profit from a takeover by a Saudi conglomerate.

The film, a dark comedy scripted by Paddy Chayefsky and directed by Sidney Lumet, is an indictment of corporate leadership, cutthroat competition, self-interest and greed. Released in 1976, it still has resonance today given the dark mirror it holds up to the business world and the pervasive influence of the media. But it also speaks to a wider audience given its focus on the effects of control, dehumanisation, grief, anxiety, alienation and loneliness. With several intertwined plot strands, it illustrates how a Collective Shadow plays out across our organisations and wider society.

By contrast, Hans Christian Andersen's fairy tale *The Shadow* is more singular in focus, exploring the effects of the Personal Shadow and how it can overwhelm us. Here, a "learned man from the cold regions becomes separated from his Shadow while spending time in a hot southern country. Many years pass, during which the Shadow enjoys both freedom and prosperity, before returning to visit his former master. As they become reacquainted, the erstwhile Shadow gradually reverses their previous roles, taking advantage of the learned man's frailty and encouraging him to act as the Shadow's own shadow. "The shadow was master now," states the narrator, "and the master became the shadow."

In each of these tales, discarded and long-hidden aspects of the protagonists' personalities resurface so powerfully that they dominate and ultimately damage not only the characters' sense of self but their relationships with other people. In *Network*, Beale is murdered on air through the machinations of network executives who seek to both remove the problem his erratic behaviour poses and boost the ratings of their shows. In *The Shadow*, fearful of being exposed by the learned man following his engagement to a princess, the Shadow triggers equally drastic action. He persuades his betrothed that the learned man is his shadow, that he has succumbed to irrecoverable madness, and that a mercy killing can be his only means of relief. Shortly before the Shadow and princess are married, the learned man is executed.

SHADOWS

Both of these tales prompt us to question whether we, too, carry Shadows within us; in what form they could manifest themselves and whether they pose a threat either to our own identity or to other people. In her essay *The Child and the Shadow*, author Ursula K. Le Guin gets to the heart of the matter in her commentary about Andersen's tale and the role played by the learned man's autonomous Shadow:

> *The shadow is all that gets suppressed in the process of becoming a decent, civilized adult. The shadow is the man's thwarted selfishness, his unadmitted desires, the swearwords he never spoke, the murders he didn't commit. The shadow is the dark side of his soul, the unadmitted, the inadmissible. And what Andersen is saying is that this monster is an integral part of the man and cannot be denied.*

With her carefully chosen words, Le Guin invokes the work of psychiatrist Carl Jung, whose ideas about human personalities, the personal unconscious and the collective unconscious draw variously on his experience in clinical practice and interest in anthropology, philosophy, mythology and analytical psychology.

Jung believed that the human psyche comprises a multiplicity rather than a single, stable identity. Everyone carries within them not only their own personal experiences, but unconscious traces of the collective human experience through time. These innate traits and characteristics common to all humankind are known as archetypes. These can be figural, like the hero figures or wise mentors of action movies, or refer to significant events and themes, like the moments of creation or apocalypse in our religious narratives. Each of our lives adds to this store of shared experiences in the collective unconscious.

Jungian therapists tell us that one of the major archetypes of the personal unconscious is the Shadow. As Le Guin suggests, the psychological interpretation of Shadows views them as repositories of all that has been repressed and pushed into the unconscious. They are shaped and informed by parental constraints and expectations during childhood, as well as cultural and social norms and our exposure to other authority figures, whether at school, in places of worship or at work.

Remaining hidden for much of the time, the Shadows occasionally show themselves in dreams and can manifest in surprising and destructive behaviour, giving expression to transgressive tendencies or deeply buried prejudices, biases and emotions. This often surfaces in public figures whose private actions contradict their carefully cultivated, respectable personas, as highlighted by the #MeToo movement's exposure of executives and celebrities engaged in sexual misconduct. But while it is natural to see narcissistic leadership embodied in polarising public figures, this often serves as a defence mechanism, allowing us to avoid confronting similar traits within ourselves.

In this way, as in Andersen's fairy tale, the Shadow archetype is often equated with darkness, even with malevolence. Nevertheless, Shadows also have come to be seen as a source of 'gifts,' such as creativity, humour and wisdom. Artists frequently show us how familiarity with the Shadows can be a rich source of inspiration and material. They find the light in the Shadows' darkness. Access to these gifts is enabled when we identify and then acknowledge the Shadows, welcome them as part of our selves and choose to work with them. It is important to maintain equilibrium, though, and avoid being swamped by the Shadows like Andersen's learned man.

A willingness to engage and collaborate with the Shadows – recognising their presence, listening to their inner voice – is commonly known as *Shadow Work*. More than a confrontation with our darker impulses, this process reveals a complex interplay of light and dark within our hidden selves. What lies concealed often surprises: unrealised creative gifts, depths of compassion never expressed, talents left dormant and joys never fully embraced exist alongside our more challenging aspects. Working with them requires delicacy, patience, care and self-reconciliation, for it is less about improving or developing ourselves than accepting the full spectrum of who we are.

As organisational development consultant Laurence Barrett explains in *A Jungian Approach to Coaching*, "We do not emerge from shadow work with a brighter light, but with a greater acceptance of the dark." This acceptance extends beyond our perceived flaws. Indeed, for many of us, our rougher edges are already on display while our more beautiful qualities remain carefully hidden. Our Shadows hold not just what we fear or reject in ourselves, but often what we dare not claim, including our capacity for love, our deepest aspirations and our most authentic expressions of self.

By welcoming our Shadows, and embracing both the darkness and the gifts they contain, we enable our own growth and move closer to self-understanding. As we will explore, Shadows are more than merely a psychological concept, but can also be understood from the perspectives of neurology, biology, physics, sociology, politics, art and philosophy. To accept our Shadows, therefore, takes us closer to knowing what it is to be human.

This is necessary work. We must understand ourselves in all our multiple dimensions before we can properly understand our colleagues, customers, friends or family. This requires us to look inward, learn to accept our whole selves, access our hidden gifts, and reconcile ourselves with whatever has the potential to derail us. For, how can we possibly inspire others to manifest their full potential if we are unable to do so ourselves?

THE FIRST STEP

"Start close in," urges poet David Whyte. "Don't take the second step or the third, start with the first thing close in, the step you don't want to take." This wisdom guides our exploration of the Shadows, those hidden aspects of ourselves that we must understand to become whole, not just as individuals but as leaders and members of an increasingly polarised society.

Shadows At Work serves as a gentle guide through the territory of Shadow Work, offering both compassion and clarity as we confront difficult truths. Through six chapters, we will explore this complex terrain. We begin with a multifaceted examination of the Shadow concept itself, proposing that it can be perceived through cultural, physiological, psychological and spiritual lenses. In subsequent chapters, we explore Projection, Defences, Derailers, Embodiment and, finally, the notion of Living the Shadow Life.

Our journey acknowledges both the darkness and the gifts within our Shadows. By engaging with, rather than neglecting, these aspects of ourselves, we can become more rounded leaders and create healthier organisations. But when we avoid this work, we risk perpetuating destructive patterns and toxicity in our teams and broader society.

This is neither a self-improvement manual nor an academic treatise. Instead, it is an invitation to those who are ready to look inward, however reluctantly. It is intended for leaders seeking to create nurturing workplaces, individuals tired of their self-sabotaging patterns and anyone willing to ask uncomfortable questions in service of growth and potential.

You may approach this material sequentially or selectively, alone or in discussion with others. My hope is that by examining how Shadows affect us – consciously and unconsciously, positively and negatively – we can develop greater understanding and compassion for ourselves and others. This is the kind of leadership our world needs now.

At the end of each chapter, you will find a selection of questions intended to prompt further reflection. Some readers may also find journaling helpful as they engage with the book's narrative. In this way, they can not only digest the theoretical insights, business stories and cultural examples, but begin to record and examine their own experiences as well.

Now, let's begin where Whyte suggests: close in, with that first challenging step.

SHADOW REFLECTIONS

- What drew you to pick up and read this book on Shadow Work?

- When you consider the word *Shadows*, what images or metaphors come to mind?

- What family, community, work and cultural systems influence you the most?

- How do these systems shape your behaviours, priorities and values?

- How have the Shadows revealed themselves in your life?

- How have they affected your work and interaction with others?

- How would you describe your relationship with your Shadows?

CHAPTER 1

LENSES

Meanings change when we receive them through different lenses.

Nora Bateson
Small Arcs of Larger Circles

Perhaps the kaleidoscope versions of ourselves that inhabit our days and nights are capable, in fact, of anything.

Doireann Ní Ghríofa
A Ghost in the Throat

Have you seen Francisco de Goya's 1799 etching *The Sleep of Reason Produces Monsters*? If not, it's worth looking for it online. A man has fallen asleep at his work table and the viewer sees the figures that populate his unconscious. It is a disturbing image, with a swirl of menacing owls and bats, suggestive of inner turmoil and fear. What Goya's work teaches us is that the Shadow is not singular but a multitude.

Shadows, in their numerous forms, are ubiquitous. Although we often lack consciousness of them, they are with us wherever we go. They impact not only our mental well-being and physical health but also how we relate to other people and our environment. "We don't perceive the world as it is," writes neuroscientist Anil Seth in *Being You*, "we perceive it as it is useful for us to do so." Shadows colour and bias our perception, as well as having a positive effect on our capacity for creativity and innovation.

What kind of challenge does this present to those exercising leadership, whether as a business executive, community leader, government official, sports coach or parent? What level of complexity is involved when we must navigate not only the effects of our own Shadows and their gifts, but those of all the people we interact with and are accountable to as well?

In this chapter, I want to raise awareness of how we think about the Shadows and loosen Jung's grip on the concept. It's not my intention to dismiss his ideas. His theories are a constant touchstone, and he will remain a lurking presence, occasionally stepping into the spotlight. But I do want to broaden how we look at the topic, taking a multidisciplinary approach.

FOUR LENSES

Shadows are not static but dynamic. As such, it is useful to consider them through several different lenses to enrich our understanding. In setting out a framework for the remainder of this book, I want to focus on four primary lenses: the cultural, the physiological, the psychological *and* the spiritual.

Each of these lenses offers *a* perspective on the Shadow. But they should not be thought wholly distinct from one another, and will be interwoven when we move on to assess how Shadows reveal themselves, the impact they have and how we can work with them. The four lenses frequently intersect, presenting an ever-shifting picture that serves up a kaleidoscopic, multidimensional view of the topic. Widespread cultural experiences are repeated in personal experiences, the physiological in the psychological, the spiritual in the cultural, and so on.

But this does not provide a complete picture. Such a study would require multiple volumes rather than this short book. Instead, what I want to do is provide us with enough to broaden our perspective and understanding. This enables is an appreciation of how patterns are repeated across a variety of theories and approaches.

Many of these hold two ideas in opposition to one another (yin/yang, light/dark, fast/slow, left/right, ground/figure, true/false, self/other) while also exploring how they interact. Where there is a greater tendency toward one side of the continuum, the more the opposing pole is pushed into the Shadows. The work involved is about recognising what we have privileged and, in turn, what we may have suppressed but which continues to affect us. This goes beyond notions of *either/or*, embracing the paradox of *both/and*.

From a leadership and organisational perspective, awareness of each of the four lenses and what they reveal is vital to effectiveness. Not only do they help improve our self-knowledge, preventing us from inadvertently acting out the worst of our Shadows, but they enhance our ability to empathise with others, to care for and guide them through their own Shadows. The lenses can help us recognise the Shadows in our organisational systems, processes and structures, providing insights about how they can be managed.

Where that does not happen, we end up with situations like the unethical leadership practices that cost Travis Kalanick his job as Uber's CEO, the emissions scandal that damaged the VW brand and the Boeing 737 MAX crisis, where executives were more interested in securing profits than addressing air safety concerns. Or, we find examples of companies or even national economies playing it safe, failing to innovate. In such cases, risk-taking and creativity are stifled, pushed into the Shadows, in favour of security and protection of the status quo. Japan, for instance, was in the vanguard of tech development but now is little more than a supporting player, having failed to stimulate start-up culture while propping up legacy enterprises.

Gestalt psychotherapist Paul McNicholls suggested that leaders and organisations should identify what they value. By examining the contrasting qualities of these attributes, they will shed light on what is suppressed, on what potentially is in the Shadows. Understanding the leader's own role in shaping and stewarding culture, and the power of their relationships with colleagues, customers and other stakeholders, is an essential starting point.

What happens when we focus on these qualities through the different lenses? What happens when we acknowledge and name them? Could they be the first steps in bringing them out of the Shadows and integrating them?

THE CULTURAL LENS

Think of culture as something that's alive. It grows and changes as people interact, share experiences and develop common values. These shared moments shape everything from family traditions to workplace habits to society's unwritten rules. If our personal Shadows represent 'the *me* I cannot see,' then looking through a cultural lens reveals 'the *we* that we cannot see.' It's like the water David Foster Wallace talked of in his celebrated 2005 commencement address at Kenyon College – it is so fundamental to our existence that we barely notice it is there.

Culture operates at different systemic levels. In organisations, subcultures can coexist within teams or parts of the same corporation. PARC, as a research subsidiary of Xerox, exemplified this. While it had its own distinctive culture of innovation and experimentation, it still operated within the parent company's broader framework. The relationship between the two cultures was complex. PARC researchers enjoyed considerable autonomy and fostered a highly creative environment, but were funded by Xerox and accountable to its corporate objectives. Xerox's more traditional corporate culture had an inhibiting effect on PARC and its ability to commercialise many of its groundbreaking innovations. Despite the research unit's groundbreaking work in computing, Xerox remained primarily a copier and printer company, hastening its slide from relevance.

Early in my career, I was an Executive Fellow at IE Business School in Madrid, where I worked with organisational theorist Gareth Jones, co-author of *Why Should Anyone Be Led By You?* He described company culture as the unwritten rules, or 'mood music,' of an organisation. He said it is something that is often discovered because of a transgression.

Jones would ask the leaders he worked with to imagine they were briefing someone new to their company about how to be successful. He would challenge them to identify the unwritten rules that should be shared with these new recruits. Their replies were revealing: "Walk around the corridors at pace, looking like you're busy." "If you go home early, leave your jacket on your chair so it looks like you've popped out for a short while." "Never get on the wrong side of Mr. Brown, as he is connected to the CEO." These Shadow rules reflected the true organisational culture, not what was codified in policies and processes or depicted on an organisational chart.

A culture weaves together a community's customs, language, art, laws and social institutions. While each community creates its own unique patterns, Jung believed there was something deeper connecting all humans. As described earlier, he referred to this as the collective unconscious (which itself has collective Shadows). It explains why we find similar themes, symbols and story patterns across different cultures. Political movements, religious beliefs, money systems and artistic expression all emerge from these cultures, and despite superficial differences, there are surprising connections that underpin them.

Psychiatrist Jacques Lacan offers a similar but distinct perspective on Jung's notion of the collective unconscious. Where Jung explores psychological and spiritual connections, Lacan focuses on language and social structures. His *symbolic order* reveals how societal norms and power dynamics inform our understanding of identity and socially acceptable behaviour, including what is pushed into the Shadows. This continues to play out in contemporary debates regarding diversity, inclusion, tolerance and so-called cancel culture. One person's identity has become another's linguistic weapon.

From a cultural perspective, one of the most significant ways in which the Shadows express themselves is through the projection of undesirable qualities onto other groups or cultures. Prejudice, discrimination, stereotyping and violence against *the other* all stem from this outward projection of what lurks internally. Not only are the inherent tendencies the culture has repressed or denied then seen in others, they also become visible through a culture's own art or, more problematically, they erupt in harmful and destructive ways within society itself. The darkness then becomes normalised.

THE PHYSIOLOGICAL LENS

The longevity of a culture relies on the inheritance of genes and memes by the next generation. This includes the passing on of Shadows as well as other characteristics, which can manifest in different ways. For example, studies of intergenerational trauma among Indigenous populations whose ancestors were subjected to brutal colonisation point to this legacy being both somatic (bodily) and psychological, encoded in the physical body as well as the unconscious mind.

Neurobiologist Robert Sapolsky's work examines cultural and evolutionary effects on humans and primates. Sapolsky highlights the darker Shadow aspects of the human experience, such as violence, aggression and stress, noting their roots in primal fight-or-flight responses to threats, territoriality and dominance. In his book *Determined*, he also draws insights from his personal experience of depression.

Sapolsky's approach emphasises the complex interplay of genetics, cultural heritage, brain chemistry and personal history in how we act or respond in any given situation. The more stressful we find it, the more likely that elevated hormone levels will prompt antisocial, impulsive or aggressive behaviour. Without effective regulation by the brain's amygdala and prefrontal cortex, we will find it difficult to override these Shadow impulses and empathise with others. We are then governed by innate biological drives and chemically induced emotions. We see and interact with the world through the state of our nervous systems.

In *My Stroke of Insight*, neuroscientist Jill Bolte Taylor elaborates on this idea: "Although many of us may think of ourselves as thinking creatures that feel, biologically we are feeling creatures that think." Sometimes, we can appear most fully ourselves when in Shadow mode, unconstrained by ego or social expectations. Our Shadow selves are not only manifestations of unconscious and hidden impulses and tendencies. As the work of Sapolsky and others reveals, they are biological, chemical and physical as well. Emotions, hormones and the nervous system all play a part, alongside environmental influences, cultural norms and evolutionary biology.

Ironically, for Taylor, the thinking mind acts as a constraining agent, limiting self-experience to the narrow confines of personality while relegating the full exuberance of *being* to the Shadows. When she suffered a stroke, and her analytical thinking was temporarily disabled, she discovered a more vivid and unencumbered experience of existence.

What Taylor underwent resonates with the perspective of author and journalist Annabel Abbs-Street, who has explored how notable writers and artists – particularly women like Virginia Woolf, Lee Krasner, Joan Mitchell, Louise Bourgeois, Katherine Mansfield and Laura Cereta – accessed their most creative work through their 'Night Selves.' Abbs-Street investigates how hormonal shifts and the nocturnal quieting of the prefrontal cortex generate chemical conditions that enable access to Shadow gifts like creative courage and artistic insight.

The exploration of Shadow creativity and psychological depths finds powerful expression in artist Edvard Munch's Expressionist painting *The Scream*. The central figure recoils in horror, hands raised to their featureless face, their anguish so profound that it appears to warp the surrounding landscape. The weight of psychological torment presses down on their skull like a physical burden. Both body and mind shudder at the raw emotional revelation.

Like a visual metaphor for the internal struggles of conscious-ness, Munch's painting prompts us to consider the complex interplay between emotion and cognition. In *Thinking, Fast and Slow*, psychologist Daniel Kahneman illuminates this by distinguishing between two essential modes of thought. System 1 is instinctive, automatic and rapid. It is Shadow-like, influenced by somatic markers, emotions, intuition, biases and unconscious mental processes. System 2 operates more slowly, employing deliberative logic and requiring conscious self-control. While Munch's figure appears overwhelmed by System 1's raw impulses, awareness of how these systems interact offers a path to greater psychological balance and adaptability.

There are fascinating parallels between Kahneman's model and psychiatrist Iain McGilchrist's neurological research. In *The Master and His Emissary*, for example, McGilchrist focuses on two distinct but interrelated modes of cognition, mapping them onto the brain's hemispheres. The *master* refers to the right hemisphere of the brain. Like System 1, it tends to be more intuitive and rapid, possessing a holistic consciousness that embodies our Shadow side. This contrasts with the analytical, reductive and deliberative approach of System 2 and the left-hemisphere *emissary*.

The left hemisphere perceives the world in fragments, abstracting and categorising, gravitating toward the mechanical, the measurable and the explicable. Its focus is on the self. Conversely, the right hemisphere prioritises experiential understanding, making connections, contextualising and perceiving systemic wholes. It demonstrates a deep capacity for empathy and care.

For modern leaders, the critical challenge lies in effectively integrating these hemispheric modes. Whether their Shadow Work focuses outwardly on organisational dynamics or inwardly on self-understanding, the goal remains the same: achieving a nuanced, balanced engagement with the complex world around them.

Physiological states like exhaustion and burnout represent another critical dimension of Shadow behaviour, with an impact on decision-making and emotions. "Fatigue makes cowards of us all," suggested General George Patton. His insight reveals how physical and mental exhaustion can affect leadership and relationships.

Modern organisational structures, with their relentless focus on productivity, often create conditions that inadvertently exacerbate Shadow behaviours. When leaders are persistently stressed, under pressure or exhausted, their capacity for measured and empathic responses diminishes. The physiological toll of such environments can trigger more reactive, less integrated modes of engagement, where intuitive impulses override rational consideration. We will return to these ideas in the chapter on Embodiment.

Writer Philip Pullman's *His Dark Materials* trilogy of fantasy novels offers a metaphorical exploration of these psychological and physiological integrations. Readers follow a quest across multiple universes that reimagines Milton's *Paradise Lost* as a battle between freedom and religious authority. One of the protagonists is Lyra Belacqua, a young girl who comes from a world where every human has a dæmon, an animal-form manifestation of their soul that stays constantly by their side. The bond between Lyra and her dæmon Pantalaimon, depicts the ideal integration between cognitive hemispheres. Pantalaimon represents the intuitive, holistic right hemisphere, while Lyra embodies the analytical, task-oriented left hemisphere.

The moment Lyra must separate from Pantalaimon to journey into the underworld serves as an allegory of fragmentation. The rupture causes intense physical and psychological trauma, mirroring McGilchrist's critique of Western societal priorities and norms, with analytical control and efficiency overshadowing emotional intelligence and holistic understanding.

Pullman's narrative holds that human potential emerges not through the dominance of one cognitive mode, but through embracing our Shadows as a vital, generative dimension of experience. Just as Lyra and Pantalaimon represent the integration of analytical and intuitive selves, we can only fully understand ourselves by recognising the Shadows not as adversaries to be feared, but essential partners in our psychological complexity.

THE PSYCHOLOGICAL LENS

Just as our physiological states and cognitive modes reveal a complex interplay of conscious and unconscious processes, the psychological lens offers further insights into the intricate landscape of the human psyche. While Sigmund Freud did not directly address the concept of the Shadow, his work on the unconscious and the repression of 'unacceptable' thoughts, feelings and desires laid foundations for subsequent psychological theories, such as those of Jung and Lacan.

Lacan's notion of the mirror stage, for example, provides a pivotal framework for understanding psychological development. Describing how infants develop a sense of self by identifying with their image in a mirror, this concept reveals a fundamental personality split. The mirror stage establishes the groundwork for an idealised mirror-ego and the repression of disavowed, alienated parts of the self. It introduces a visual dimension to our understanding of psychological perception.

Building on this visual metaphor, Gestalt psychology, which emphasises comprehension of organised wholes rather than individual parts, distinguishes between the *figure* and the *ground* to illuminate the notion of psychological perception. We naturally focus on the figure (the central, conscious element) while the ground represents the surrounding context and unconscious elements. Colour, size, separation and contour influence how we differentiate one from the other. When we observe *The Scream*, for example, our attention is immediately drawn to the central figure positioned in the foreground. We then become aware of the background figures, the boats and the swirling ground against which the figure is clearly defined.

Just as the ground in Gestalt psychology reveals what lies beneath the surface, developmental psychology explores how our hidden, unconscious self develops through early interactions. Psychoanalyst Donald Winnicott introduced the notion of the *true self* and the *false self*. The latter emerges as a protective mechanism, a social mask that represses our natural impulses and adapts to external expectations. Like a performative social media avatar, the false self develops in response to childhood experiences, hiding the whole self and what is deemed unacceptable.

Throughout childhood and adolescence, we are shaped by the roles played by caregivers, family, friends and society. We quickly learn which behaviours and emotional expressions are acceptable, internalising these lessons and contributing to the formation of our Shadow. Jung's concept of the *persona*, which is derived from the Latin for 'mask' and rooted in ancient Greek theatrical traditions, illuminates how we construct social identities and roles.

Infants initially act on pure instinct, with no awareness of social expectations. As children grow, they observe and imitate behaviours, learning social norms through play and interaction. Each time a child's genuine expression is rejected or punished, aspects of their personality are pushed into the Shadows. A child who is told not to cry, sing or express certain emotions learns to suppress these natural impulses.

In adolescence and adulthood, these personas become more complex. We develop different sub-personalities for various life contexts. We can present very different versions of ourselves at work, with friends and with family. While these masks help with social adaptation, they can also lead to a disconnection from our authentic selves.

Research shared by psychologist James Fadiman and writer Jordan Gruber in *Your Symphony of Selves* highlights how we are composed of multiple selves, each with distinct desires, abilities and perspectives. We might experience this as the focused professional self who excels at work, the playful self who emerges with close friends or the nurturing self who cares for family members. Sometimes these selves compete; sometimes they collaborate. For instance, our disciplined, athletic self might come into conflict with our comfort-seeking self, while our creative and analytical selves might work together to solve complex problems. Recognising this complexity can foster greater self-compassion and understanding of our internal conflicts. But the alternative to acknowledging our Shadows is a fragmented psyche, leaving us trapped in a hall of mirrors, unable to grasp our true nature.

The process of *individuation,* which is a core concept in Jungian psychology, involves a lifelong journey through which we become fully integrated, unique individuals. This goes beyond mere personal growth, representing a process of self-discovery where we consciously confront and reconcile the various aspects of our psyches, including our Shadows. When we accept the interactive tension between our conscious personas and our unconscious Shadows, we can move toward a more authentic and holistic understanding of our psychological landscape, embracing the complexity of our inner worlds rather than fragmenting or denying them.

We will explore the psychological lens further when we examine how Shadow behaviour emerges in the form of projection, defences and derailers. But it should be noted that the quest for wholeness extends beyond the psychological realm, inviting us to explore deeper dimensions of human experience. The journey of understanding our Shadows does not end with psychological insight but opens an opportunity for broader spiritual contemplation.

THE SPIRITUAL LENS

It is through the spiritual lens that meaning and purpose become visible. Traditionally, this has been the realm of mythology, passed-down wisdom, depth psychology, mysticism, contemplative practices, religion, art and the poetic. Yet, spirituality cannot be divorced from any other aspect of life. It is present when the scientist conducts experiments and encounters the awe of nature, when the artist applies brush strokes to the canvas, when the comedian reveals deep truths through poignant wit.

How we define spirituality may differ according to our preferred disciplines, practices and belief systems, but each enables greater understanding of our personal and collective Shadows. Ironically, it is in the spiritual and religious traditions that emphasise the 'light' that Shadows have tended to erupt in their darkest forms: child abuse, cover-ups, embezzlement, excessive control of the vulnerable. Many claiming to embody the good have been found to have feet of clay.

The spiritual dimension of Shadow Work reveals itself most powerfully in our quest for meaning and purpose. In the world of work, this manifests as a deeper inquiry. Why do we do what we do? What defines success beyond mere professional achievement? These questions speak to our hunger for significance. During my time in investment banking, I witnessed this yearning firsthand. When I organised a talk on 'Meaning at Work,' nearly 200 people signed up within minutes. This was a testament to people's deep desire to understand their professional lives through a more holistic lens.

This search for meaning, however, can become a trap if not approached with genuine self-awareness. The psychotherapist John Welwood coined the term *spiritual bypassing* to describe how individuals use supernatural ideas to avoid confronting unresolved psychological wounds. While such avoidance might provide temporary comfort, it ultimately leads to a fragmented self. True spiritual growth requires us to engage directly with our Shadows, integrating rather than avoiding the darker aspects of our experience.

My own journey illustrates this challenge. Initially trained in transpersonal psychotherapy, I found myself drawn to vertical development, exploring spiritual and meditative practices. Yet, I soon realised that what I truly needed was horizontal development, focusing on relationships and everyday experiences. This shift led me to Gestalt psychology, which emphasises *the here and now*. It helped me redefine my understanding by acknowledging that I grow in my spirituality by growing in my humanity. It is not about transcending human experience, but fully inhabiting it.

The teachings of the 13th century mystic and theologian Meister Eckhart also have proved to be hugely influential for me. "Truly, it is in the darkness that one finds the light," he wrote, "so when we are in sorrow, then this light is nearest of all to us." He and other Christian mystics, like St. John of the Cross, author of *The Dark Night of the Soul*, emphasise the importance of going deep into the darkness, our Shadows and the mystery of the self to achieve a spiritual awakening and transformation. Finding and realising our essence can only be achieved through a journey of *descent*, going beyond the superficiality of ego, dogma and social conditioning.

Eastern spiritual traditions also emphasise the integration of the darkness. From Taoism we discover that the Shadows are an intrinsic part of our true nature. Yin and yang are interdependent and inseparable aspects of an undivided whole, each containing aspects of the other. However, where balance is not maintained, the interaction between yin and yang is disturbed and creates disharmony.

We learn that we must recognise both our Shadows and our light. Neither is present without the other. Failing to acknowledge this can adversely affect both individuals and organisations. The disharmony manifests as ill health, dysfunction, incivility, aggression, lethargy and an inability to adapt to change. Significantly, when we neglect the light hidden in the Shadows, we neglect the gifts we can bring into our lives and work. This is the most tragic cost of avoiding Shadow Work.

Buddhism offers another perspective. Here, Shadows are understood to be transitional energies related to undesirable characteristics like greed, hatred and delusion. As there is no fixed self with which these Shadows can be integrated, the work relies on insight, recognising these energies, accepting them and then letting them go. The focus is on presence in the moment, which means that, unlike with many psychological or therapeutic approaches, there is little concern with historical Shadow formation in the individual's or organisation's past.

This Buddhist approach of present-moment awareness and non-attachment resonates with a deeper understanding of human experience, one that embraces interconnectedness and wholeness. Like the wisdom found in contemplative traditions, I have found that poetry can offer great insights into our relationship with darkness and light. The poet Wendell Berry invites us to consider this integration, suggesting that our fragmented experiences can be understood not as separate parts, but as a unified, living landscape of being. In *The Peace of Wild Things*, his narrator observes:

> *I come into the peace of wild things*
> *who do not tax their lives with forethought*
> *of grief. I come into the presence of still water.*
> *And I feel above me the day-blind stars*
> *waiting with their light. For a time*
> *I rest in the grace of the world, and am free.*

Berry's poem speaks of the benefits and gifts that can come from life's difficulties and sorrows. It provides us with another perspective with which to approach Goya's *The Sleep of Reason Produces Monsters*. The paintbrushes on the worktable suggest that the sleeping figure is an artist. Could he be 'resting in grace,' harnessing his creative gifts while in communion with his Shadows? Rather than symbolising the fears that will consume him, could the creatures we see represent the artistic inspiration he will experience upon awakening?

As illustrated by another of his poems, *To Know the Dark*, Berry was all too aware of the gifts that could be found in the Shadows:

> *To go in the dark with a light is to know the light.*
> *To know the dark, go dark. Go without sight,*
> *and find that the dark, too, blooms and sings,*
> *and is traveled by dark feet and dark wings.*

The four lenses provide us with tools to do something similar, unearthing what is hidden, bringing it into the light and consciously making it our own.

SHADOW REFLECTIONS

- Can you find examples in your own life of Shadow behaviour under each of the lenses?

- Which lens are you most curious about? Why?

- Which of the lenses are currently most dominant in your life?

- Which are the personas you most frequently use?

- Do you over-identify with any of them?

- Which are you less familiar with, having pushed them into the Shadows?

SHADOWS REVEALED

**Hello darkness, my old friend
I've come to talk with you again**

Simon & Garfunkel
The Sound of Silence

Shadow work is not about improving or reconstructing ourselves. The steps we take are gentle ones: accepting ourselves, befriending our worst traits.

David Richo
Shadow Dance

Sometimes, through our dreams, our Shadows offer us glimpses of alternative lives we could lead, and we find ourselves acting in ways that we would not dare contemplate when conscious. At night, the nurse becomes a serial killer, the bank clerk a thief, the teacher a despot and the introvert a superhero.

What happens, though, when Shadows suddenly erupt into our waking lives?

> *Rachel was ambitious. She wanted recognition and success, as well as the rewards and status that would accompany them. But when she was put forward for promotion and her objective was within reach, Rachel started behaving in unexpected ways that damaged her prospects. Where normally she was attentive and punctual, now she procrastinated, missed deadlines and was curt with colleagues. She began to question her own worth and capabilities, suddenly fearing failure and ducking responsibility. Rachel's drop in performance and unusual irascibility were noted. She did not get the job, having been derailed by her own Shadows.*

What happens when our Shadows remain unacknowledged?

> *From a young age, Mo's potential as a highly skilled tennis player had been recognised and nurtured by his enthusiastic father. While Mo was a brilliant professional, he repeatedly found ways to sabotage his chances of success. At the slightest provocation, he would lose his self-control, venting his anger and frustration in outbursts directed at officials, opponents and spectators, or in violent assaults on tennis racquets and balls. Inevitably, this would affect his technique and concentration. His body would stiffen and he would lose his sense of flow, resulting in the frequent loss of*

*matches he should have won. Mo realised that he had
been living a Shadow career, one that he was deeply
unhappy with and that did not reflect his own desires,
despite the occasional tournament success.*

What happens when our leaders' Shadows negatively impact
organisational culture?

*Javier was a respected leader known for his fairness.
But as he acquired more power, eventually becoming
CEO, he exhibited greater entitlement and self-
obsession. Javier was convinced that he was always
right, that the decisions he made were well-founded
and not open to question. Nevertheless, many of
his initiatives didn't go well. When confronting his
executives, reporting to the board or sharing his
discontent on social media, Javier was quick to blame
others for these failures. While he appeared immune
to the external scrutiny his public pronouncements
attracted and to the confusion caused by his
contradictory internal edicts, Javier's senior colleagues
had to pick up the pieces. His anger and finger-pointing
cascaded down through the organisation, poisoning
its culture. Many talented people left the company,
while a few unfortunate scapegoats were fired. Those
who remained kept their heads down for fear of being
singled out.*

What happens when we find the gifts in our Shadows and learn
to integrate them into our lives?

*Kamila had learned from an early age that if she
questioned social and cultural norms, she could
expect reprisals. Because she lived in fear of violent
punishment, she conformed to what was expected of her.
Yet, the more she witnessed injustice and inequality,*

the more she felt compelled to speak out. Eventually,
Kamila confronted and embraced her fears, using them
to fuel her new-found activism and encourage others
to follow suit. She realised that she was connected to,
and in service of, a higher purpose. This enabled her to
transform her long-held fears into strengths, catalysing
a movement that would speak truth to power and
campaign for change.

When involved in Shadow Work, we will constantly encounter an array of challenging questions and scenarios that demand our attention. Establishing an understanding of how Shadows are manifested, what impact they can have and how we can constructively engage with them is vital to the effectiveness of our personal and professional development.

While Shadow Work improves our self-awareness, it also helps us become attuned to cultural and personal nuances. We learn to appreciate how others communicate not only through words but with their silences, gestures and bodies, both as individuals and as participants in larger systems. Like a detective, we must constantly look for clues, using the multiple lenses to assess the combined effects of psychological, physiological, cultural and spiritual factors.

Shadow Work is not a methodical process of illumination, like shining a flashlight into a darkened room and attempting to piece together a comprehensive view. It is not a self-improvement technique aimed at identifying and changing sources of discontent. Instead, it is about being present within the darkness, allowing our perception to gradually adjust, learning to see and understand without forcing immediate transformation.

This work is inherently challenging, and we must accept that we may falter many times before we become reconciled with our Personal and Collective Shadows. Self-forgiveness, tolerance and compassion will help smooth the way. But we must recognise that our Shadows are formed and healed through our relationships, requiring a gentle, compassionate and sometimes playful approach.

It is essential that we do not treat Shadows as if they were external entities to be managed and controlled. The linguistic tendency to speak of Shadows as something separate can perpetuate the very mechanism of disconnection that originally created these hidden aspects of ourselves. Our goal is not to accept or integrate Shadows as foreign objects, but to acknowledge them as essential components of our whole self.

But this is not a linear journey. We might believe we have accepted and integrated a particular Shadow aspect, only to find ourselves repeating old patterns. Things may often feel more complicated or intense before they begin to improve. When we become aware of our Shadows, we confront parts of ourselves that, previously, were avoided or left unexplored.

Shadow Work is ultimately about choice. We can choose to engage with these hidden parts of ourselves, not through force or judgement, but through curious, compassionate awareness. This is about recognising that our Shadows are not our enemies, but messengers carrying insights about our deeper selves.

Confronting and working productively with our Shadows is not easy, but it is deeply rewarding. It offers us the opportunity to move from a state of unconscious reactivity to one of conscious, integrated wholeness.

CHAPTER 2

PROJECTION

Elaborate are the means to hide from yourself, the disassociations, projections, deceptions, forgettings, justifications, and other tools to detour around the obstruction of unbearable reality, the labyrinths in which we hide the minotaurs who have our faces.

Rebecca Solnit
The Faraway Nearby

The path to the truth is doubled, masked, ironic. This is my path, not straight, but twisted!

Siri Hustvedt
The Blazing World

Have you ever been on the receiving end of a finger-pointing rant or involved in an argument where everything the other person is accusing you of seems to describe their own faults and biases? Have you ever found yourself doing the same thing – perhaps not in the moment, but when tempers have cooled and you have had a chance to reflect on what happened?

Have you ever idolised someone while simultaneously sensing your own lack or inferiority? Or, have you experienced disappointment when those you hold in high esteem have behaved in ways that do not meet your expectations?

For Freud, the psychological concept of *projection* is a defence mechanism that enables us to avoid directly confronting those aspects of ourselves that we deem unacceptable. It protects us from uncomfortable truths. Instead, we attribute our unconscious thoughts, feelings and traits to others, seeing in them negative characteristics that we possess. Because our view of the world is egocentric, distorted by our own subjectivity, we see our shortcomings manifest in the people around us. From the Freudian perspective, projection is a symptom of psychological conflict or pathology.

For my own part, following one job change, I discovered projection's revelatory power. I had moved recently to a new functional area in my company and immediately perceived a new colleague as detached and exclusionary. I believed he intentionally withheld information, avoided me in meetings and had adopted a competitive stance in his relationship with me. I was convinced he felt threatened by my presence. However, after deep reflection, I realised that every criticism I levelled at him was, in fact, a precise description of my own unconscious behaviour.

I was the one who had been aloof, who had avoided scheduling regular catch-ups and who had been hesitant to share information. Whatever threats I perceived did not emanate from him, but from my own unacknowledged insecurities. This experience repeated a pattern from my childhood, where I had competed with a younger sibling, jealous of the attention shown him, fearful of being displaced. Unconsciously, I was still trying to prove my worth and manage anything I thought threatened me.

"We don't see things as they are," the writer Anaïs Nin observed, "we see things as we are." This is the essence of projection. The external world becomes a screen upon which we unconsciously project our internal landscape. In workplace contexts, this manifests in myriad ways. For example, an employee who constantly accuses colleagues of taking credit might themselves be secretly yearning for recognition, while a leader who micromanages might be projecting their own fear of inadequacy onto their employees.

Theatre provides a powerful illustration of projection's destructive potential. In Shakespeare's tragedy *Othello*, the protagonist, at Iago's devious prompting, projects all his own anxieties and insecurities onto his innocent wife Desdemona. Increasingly convinced of her infidelity, Othello loses self-control and murders her. Iago plays on Othello's sense of otherness to manipulate both what he sees and feels. The latter gradually loses his grip on reality, blinkered by what his mind colours and distorts as it is projected onto the world around him.

While such a dramatic example highlights the devastating way in which projection can work, the process is far more complex than a simple defence against uncomfortable truths. Psychological theories offer increasingly sophisticated understandings of how and why we project our inner experiences onto others. A Jungian understanding is particularly nuanced. Here, projection is a means for the unconscious to communicate with the conscious as a normal part of psychological development and interpersonal relationships.

Object Relations Theory (ORT), pioneered by psychoanalyst Melanie Klein, further illuminates this intricate psychological process. ORT proposes that we internalise our early relationships, creating mental representations of ourselves and others. However, while a normal feature of childhood development, splitting off parts of the self prevents us from having a holistic view of the world, enforcing a polarising perspective. We cannot accept that someone can possess both 'good' and 'bad' qualities; they must either be *all* good or *all* bad.

This concept of splitting intersects with the notions of Shadow formation and projection. If we are to perceive ourselves as either all good or all bad, then we use a defensive mechanism to split off and suppress the opposite qualities, unconsciously projecting them onto others, and protecting against anxiety and conflict. For Klein, mature development involves the integration of these split perceptions. For Jung, it necessitates the recognition of what has been projected and its conscious reintegration into the psyche.

In Patricia Highsmith's novel *The Talented Mr. Ripley*, Tom Ripley's unstable identity stems from a troubled childhood during which he was orphaned and largely neglected by the aunt tasked with raising him. He associates lack of money and low social status with his aunt, believing them to be 'bad' qualities. This motivates his own criminal behaviour as a counterfeiter and conman, as well as his use of projection as a defence mechanism and means of self-transformation.

While in Italy, Tom projects his own desires and aspirations onto the privileged Dickie Greenleaf. He envies Dickie's wealth and social status, picturing himself living Dickie's life. Tom's fabrications, manipulation of other people and self-deception ultimately lead him to murder and impersonate Dickie, continuing the lavish lifestyle he has begun to enjoy at the expense the Greenleaf family. He defends himself against threats to this masquerade, projecting the worst of himself onto Freddie Miles, who becomes another of his murder victims.

By the latter stages of the book, Tom has resumed his own identity to protect himself against police investigation and to deflect the suspicions of Dickie's girlfriend, Marge Sherwood. But there is a sense that this identity never stabilises, and remains fragmented. Tom ends the novel having inherited Dickie's fortune because of a will he forged, but beset by paranoia and anxiety. He continues to idealise what Dickie had and devalue his own existence and heritage. Maturity and integration remain beyond his reach.

PROJECTIVE IDENTIFICATION

In *The Unwanted Self*, their study of the effects of Shadow behaviours on organisational leadership, business school academics Gianpiero Petriglieri and Mark Stein adopt Klein's term *projective identification*. They argue that in seeking to align themselves with a desirable leadership identity, or 'wanted self,' there is a tendency among leaders to project undesirable or 'unwanted' selves and their respective characteristics onto colleagues and business rivals.

By the same token, leaders may *introject* (take in) the expectations placed on them by the positive projections of their followers, assimilating them into an idealised leadership identity that they seek to adopt. Like actors on the stage, they practice an 'as if' persona, giving expression to traits, characteristics and abilities that they may not possess yet but wish to develop. This is reflective of the 'fake it till you make it' mindset that has dominated business culture for decades and is especially prevalent in start-up environments.

However, the possible ways leaders can show up then become limited. Richard Olivier, co-founder of the Olivier Mythodrama leadership development consultancy, with its Archetypes at Work process, suggested that some may find they can only bring a few leadership archetypes onto the stage while pushing others into the wings. There is a danger, then, that they develop strengths in only one or two leadership personas, over-using and over-relying on them. Eventually, their leadership style becomes less fluid, and they are unable to adapt to new contexts. Some leaders, for example, may be so used to having a coaching and collaborative style that they are incapable of being directive when it is called for.

When leaders restrict their leadership styles to a few personas, projective identification can exacerbate the situation, creating further psychological and organisational challenges. While it can reduce a leader's inner turmoil and enable them to confront and control what they perceive as threatening, it also can impact organisational culture, employee performance, decision-making and their own effectiveness. This is especially the case when conflict arises between the leaders and those onto whom they have projected their undesirable traits or unrealistic and one-sided perspectives. The breakdown of relationships can have far-reaching consequences, as we will see when we address the topic of scapegoating.

But it also can be highly problematic when leaders are judged by whatever others have projected onto them. These projections can highlight collective biases. Gender disparities are evident, for example, when decisive and directive male leaders are seen as *assertive*, but their female counterparts are labelled *bossy*. There is also a risk that staff and other stakeholders can succumb to hero worship, seeing their own ideals and aspirations manifested in the identity assumed by the leader.

In *Fake Heroes*, political journalist Otto English argues that many historical figures who have been celebrated for their heroism, from Mother Theresa to Che Guevara, have been misrepresented. Their glorification is simplistic. It fails to account for the discrepancy between the mask that has been donned and the leader's own complex identity, which is more multifaceted than those who laud them allow for. This could be observed, for example, in the way acolytes responded to Steve Jobs's charismatic leadership of Apple, blind to what more detached observers referred to as the 'reality distortion field' he created around himself, the company and its products, as well as his poor treatment of colleagues and family.

We need to be cautious about who we idolise. The heroes we admire often have back stories and have made sacrifices that few of us would want to emulate. Take Elon Musk, for instance, who is lauded as the world's richest man and celebrated for his leadership in technological innovation and at companies like Tesla and SpaceX. Yet, how many would truly want his lifestyle? The 100-hour work weeks, sleeping on factory floors or in cars, abrupt dismissals via impersonal communication channels – these are not typically aspirational life choices. Admiration can gloss over alarming behaviour that has intensified as his power has grown. It has included puerile social media spats and amplification of far-right and populist groups, as well as more troubling actions since briefly joining Trump's administration in early 2025. Musk has been seen making perceived Nazi salutes and wielding a chainsaw on stage, even as he has orchestrated the mass firing of U.S. Federal Government employees. Celebrated public personae often conceal patterns of conduct that contradict professed personal values.

Another risk is that leaders themselves fall prey to the saviour complex. This psychological condition compels them to rescue others, solving their problems or leading them to a perceived promised land, even when there is no consent on the part of those being 'saved.' Leadership expert Simon Western, founder of The Eco-Leadership Institute, argues that fulfilling the role of an idealised saviour is both a cultural power play and a social defence mechanism. In humanitarian contexts, this can lead to organisations objectifying and depersonalising those they aim to help. Aid workers may unconsciously project their own vulnerabilities – fear, helplessness, anxiety – onto the populations they serve, stripping away individual agency and simplifying contextual complexity.

Another recent example of the saviour complex is provided by Elizabeth Holmes, founder of the health technology start-up Theranos. Holmes had a grandiose vision of her company revolutionising blood testing and transforming healthcare. However, she was so single-minded in attempting to realise this vision that she dismissed criticism, allowed ethical compromises and engaged in fraudulent practices. This resulted in the company's dissolution and Holmes's imprisonment.

Something similar happened with Sam Bankman-Fried's involvement in the cryptocurrency industry and his 'poster child' role for the socio-philosophical movement *effective altruism*. Bankman-Fried claimed he was pursuing a high-paying career with the aim of donating a significant proportion of his income to progressive causes, where maximum good could be achieved through reason-based decision-making and action. Lauded by investors as a visionary hero and celebrated by the media for his entrepreneurial capabilities and philanthropy, he was soon vilified for mismanagement of the digital currency exchange FTX Trading and misuse of customer funds. Bankman-Fried was convicted of fraud and sentenced to 25 years in prison.

There is something in both Holmes's and Bankman-Fried's cases that tells us more about the Silicon Valley culture in which they operated than about the individuals themselves. We must remain suspicious of and resistant to the collective need to project halos or devil horns onto people. Each situation is usually far more nuanced than the portrayal of someone as all good or all bad would suggest. But Silicon Valley sees itself as a tech utopia in which fantasies and projections mingle. It is where immense sums of money and the desire for 'unicorn' status shape behaviours and outcomes. While failures are common, so are the inflated egos that parallel the inflated valuations of businesses and projects.

This tendency to oversimplify and categorise extends beyond the tech world to other spheres, with the U.S. Elections of 2024 offering a recent example. Some pundits noted how the left's demonising of Donald Trump backfired, contributing to the Democratic Party's defeat. In a podcast conversation with pop-culture interviewer Joe Rogan, Trump revealed a more layered personality than many of the one-dimensional caricatures of him would suggest. This attracted voters who did not necessarily agree with his policies but could relate to him on a human level.

The need to flatten complex narratives into simplistic caricatures is more than a superficial media phenomenon. It reflects a deeper psychological mechanism through which we project, categorise and distance ourselves from the uncomfortable complexities of human nature. But what happens when leaders not only become trapped by external projections, but actively internalise and embody their most destructive impulses?

THE MONSTER'S JOURNEY

Throughout history, leaders have exhibited a disturbing tendency to suppress their 'good' qualities while amplifying their 'bad' ones. The unwanted self can gradually become the dominant self, sometimes permanently transforming an individual.

The 20th century provides many examples of this psychological phenomenon. Dictatorial figures like Hitler, Mussolini, Stalin, Franco, Idi Amin, Pol Pot, Mugabe and Pinochet illustrate how personal darkness can infect national cultures. Each followed a trajectory toward the monstrous. Hitler, for example, was an aspiring artist who became the driving force behind Nazi Germany's atrocities. Similarly, Robert Mugabe transformed from a principled African Nationalist and anti-colonialist to a power-hungry authoritarian after Zimbabwe's independence.

These historical figures continue to cast long shadows. Their crimes stand as uncomfortable reminders of humanity's potential for moral corruption. But during a conversation with philosopher Bayo Akomolafe, I encountered a provocative perspective on these seemingly monstrous figures. He argued that they serve a deeper psychological purpose.

Such figures challenge our assumptions about human nature, Akomolafe suggested. They force us to confront uncomfortable truths about ourselves by shattering conventional narratives of good and evil. Their polarising presence offers a deceptive simplicity in an increasingly complex world. This pattern can also be seen in how we treat our cultural icons, including business leaders, athletes and celebrities. We elevate these figures to almost mythical status, constructing narratives of perfection. Inevitably, when their human flaws emerge, we experience a visceral need to tear down their carefully constructed pedestals, transforming our former heroes into monsters.

Just as mythology describes a Hero's Journey, there is also a Monster's Journey, which is equally informative. This reveals how even the most venerated people can undergo radical moral transformations. Every hero can become a monster.

Aung San Suu Kyi, for example, was once celebrated globally as a Nobel Peace Prize laureate and symbol of resistance against Myanmar's military regime. She later became a defender of the very violence she once opposed. Her story illustrates how public projection can obscure human complexity. As her actions diverged from the idealistic expectations of those who championed her, the disconnect became impossible to ignore. Her dramatic fall from grace was a testament to the dangerous power of collective mythmaking.

Confronting our own potential for darkness is a fundamental act of psychological maturity, recognising that each of us has the capacity for monstrosity. Self-awareness, therefore, offers a critical lens through which we can understand our projections, seeing in others those qualities we have repressed or denied within ourselves.

There is wisdom in the adage, 'If you can spot it, you've got it.' But it is an insight that can be dangerously manipulated, particularly in the context of emotional abuse. Gaslighting, the deceitful manoeuvring of someone into doubting their own perception of reality, weaponises projection. A harmful actor can dismissively claim that their victim is 'just projecting,' effectively negating their legitimate concerns. Such tactics can undermine someone's sense of stability, stirring up self-doubt and shame.

Detecting our own projections demands the careful examination of our emotional responses. When our reactions seem disproportionate to the situation, it is possible that we are dealing with an instance of projection. *Why does this person's actions*

make me so angry? Why is my body responding so viscerally?
These are important questions that invite deeper reflection.

We have all encountered people who trigger instant and intense responses, who set our teeth on edge. They include the micromanaging boss who causes frustration, the boastful colleague who makes our eyes roll, the workplace bully whose sarcastic barbs spark inner rage, the messy housemate who embodies everything we despise or a politician whose mere appearance has us shouting at the screen. These are not random annoyances, but potential windows into our own unexamined psychological landscape.

When we find ourselves emotionally ensnared in this way, something deeper is in play. We become *hooked*, unable to look away, trapped in a reactive pattern that requires exploration. We must learn to transform our initial fury into genuine curiosity. *When have I experienced similar feelings before? In what context? In whose company?* By accepting that our most intense irritations might reflect our own unacknowledged characteristics, we open the door to Shadow Work. This is not about self-condemnation, but about compassionate self-understanding.

The contemporary impulse to create safe spaces and issue trigger warnings, while well-intentioned, can inadvertently shield us from the very experiences that might prompt self-discovery. By constantly protecting ourselves from challenging encounters, we risk missing the transformative potential of confronting our own Shadows and what they tell us about our whole selves.

MIMETIC DESIRE AND SCAPEGOATING

The human mind is a hive of complex unconscious processes that shape how we perceive ourselves and others, influencing the construction of our identities and social relationships. Projection is one of these processes. As a defence mechanism, it reflects our hidden selves, including our own shortcomings.

Mimetic desire, a concept promoted by social philosopher René Girard, takes this a step further. It suggests that our desires, behaviours and attitudes often are not original but imitative. We do not want things because of their inherent value, but because someone else wants them. Modern marketing is a testament to this psychological principle. Advertisers do not just sell products, they sell the idea that others desire these products.

Projection and mimetic desire intersect in fascinating ways. Both reveal that our sense of self is deeply relational. We define ourselves not in isolation, but through constant comparison and interaction with others. This creates a complex dynamic of simultaneous attraction and rivalry. Scapegoating emerges as a particularly destructive manifestation of these psychological processes. It is a collective defence mechanism where communities resolve internal tensions by identifying and persecuting *the other*. It involves projecting a group's collective anxieties, failures and unresolved conflicts onto a vulnerable individual or population.

For example, in a struggling start-up, a product development team faces mounting pressure after a series of missed deadlines and product launch failures. Instead of examining systemic issues, such as unrealistic timelines, inadequate resources and poor communication, senior management blame a single project manager for all the problems, publicly criticising them and terminating their employment. But by focusing on one individual, the executives avoid confronting deeper organisational dysfunction. The project manager becomes a convenient fall guy, absorbing the collective frustration and allowing the leadership team to maintain the illusion that their processes are sound.

This pattern of institutional blame-shifting is evident in real-world corporate scandals. At Theranos, for instance, the company's leadership gave a classic scapegoating response when their fraudulent practices were exposed. Elizabeth Holmes and company president Ramesh Balwani attempted to deflect responsibility by blaming laboratory directors for the ethical failures that were, in fact, entirely of their own making. Similarly, during the VW emissions scandal, senior executives sought to protect themselves by blaming a small group of engineers for what had happened. They were willing to sacrifice the credibility and skills of these formerly valued individuals to preserve their corporate brand.

At Boeing, on the other hand, scapegoats were identified outside the company, with airline pilots and maintenance crews blamed for problems with the 737 MAX aircraft that resulted in 346 deaths in two separate incidents. It was only because of the work of external investigators and the disclosures of internal whistleblowers that the company was forced to accept that design flaws in its own Maneuvering Characteristics Augmentation System (MCAS) were at fault, and that senior personnel were culpable. The scandal eventually cost CEO Dennis Muilenburg his job. From seeking to identify scapegoats, he became one himself.

True leadership and personal growth emerge from confronting challenging psychological realities. This means developing the courage to recognise our own unconscious projections, understand the mimetic nature of our desires and take collective responsibility for systemic problems. Instead of seeking quick blame, adaptive leaders create environments that welcome respectful challenge and deep self-reflection. By cultivating this approach, we can transform potentially divisive situations into opportunities for genuine understanding and collaborative improvement.

The goal is not to eliminate conflict or difference, but to develop a more nuanced understanding of how psychological mechanisms shape our social realities. When we can recognise the subtle ways projection, mimetic desire and the impulse to scapegoat operate, we become capable of building more empathetic, resilient communities that address root causes rather than symptoms.

It takes courage to speak up against these tendencies, but this is a true act of leadership. In light of this, leadership scholars Ronald Heifetz and Marty Linsky encourage adaptive leaders to question what role they have played in any mess, addressing the situation from both a personal and systemic perspective. This allows them to depersonalise the situation, identifying shared failures and opportunities for improvement rather than singling out one person or group to name and shame.

Questioning and respectful challenge can prevent us from quickly jumping to conclusions and apportioning blame. In the film *12 Angry Men*, for example, one juror challenges the certainties held by the rest of the group. By introducing doubt and offering an alternative perspective, he gradually wins them over and changes their verdict.

We may feel relief when somebody else has taken the fall. Even more so when justice appears to be done. But if root causes are not addressed, the inclination to project and scapegoat will persist.

MISATTRIBUTION

When is projection not projection? Have you ever been in a situation where, because of the similarity of a name or physical appearance, you have had someone else's traits and beliefs attributed to you?

Clearly, in scapegoating situations, it can be difficult to accept and internalise a pariah status, although it is possible to feel victimised and either reconcile yourself to the situation or react against it. In different circumstances, however, we feel compelled to reject how other people describe us. This can especially be the case when, in a Dr. Jekyll and Mr. Hyde scenario, everything we stand for and do contrasts starkly with the beliefs and actions of our counterpart.

In her book *Doppelganger*, social activist Naomi Klein explains how such an experience impacted her own life, using this as a springboard to examine the political and psychological confusion that afflicts modern society.

Klein holds a professorship in Climate Justice and has long been associated with the political left. She is known for her feminism, and her ongoing critique of neoliberal economics and the resurgence of the far right. Nevertheless, a shared first name and Jewish heritage have resulted in Klein frequently being confused with journalist and political consultant Naomi Wolf, with the latter's public pronouncements mistakenly attributed to her in both traditional and social media.

Wolf initially entered the public consciousness as a prominent feminist, launching her career with the publication of *The Beauty Myth*. But, more recently, she has become known for her advocacy of conspiracy theories, spread of misinformation and selective presentation and occasional distortion of the facts in her academic research and publications.

Having previously worked for leading U.S. Democrats like Bill Clinton and Al Gore, Wolf now tends to be bracketed with those on the right of the political spectrum. Most of Wolf's public pronouncements, therefore, are anathema to Klein. It is as if her own Shadow were taking to the stage, a figure of darkness cast into the public arena.

Klein uses the repeated confusion of identity between herself and Wolf to highlight social divisions and polarisation, as well as their amplification by social media. She addresses issues relating to the future of democracy, the rise of authoritarianism and the way fractures in society have been magnified by the financial crisis that began in 2007 and government responses to the Covid-19 pandemic.

She examines how social media serves to proliferate conspiracy theories and misinformation, blurring the boundaries between truth and fiction, with both personal and societal consequences. Social media algorithms create echo chambers that reinforce the beliefs of like-minded people but stigmatise those who do not share their views. They become arenas for scapegoating and public shame, providing an impersonal, technological means for us to project our Shadows onto what she calls "machine-made doppelgangers." Her analysis questions how the divisions can be both navigated and healed.

Klein's reflections suggest that we have a sense of who we are, but no say in how others perceive and define us. When confronted with misattribution or projection, the most constructive approach is to resist defensiveness. However unfair another person's opinion of us may be, it can reveal more about them than about us. How they respond to us has much to do with their own Shadows, shaped by the web of relationships, history and culture in which they are entangled. Nevertheless, it is important to remain open to the possibility that there might be a kernel of truth in their perception.

The self-inquiry method developed by personal-development author Byron Katie offers a valuable framework for navigating these situations. For example, if someone accuses us of lying, Katie suggests stepping back from immediate indignation and instead reflecting on moments when we *have* lied. She advocates not resisting a projection or accusation, but genuinely searching internally for where we have displayed the quality or behaviour we seem most affronted by. *When have I been arrogant, lied, cheated?*

In this way, we can acknowledge that we are not blameless, recognising that we tend to judge others on their behaviour and ourselves on our intentions. This approach transforms potential conflict into an opportunity for self-reflection. The goal is not to come from a place of blind acceptance or denial, but to listen with openness, taking on board what is useful and discerning what is not relevant to us.

SELF-PROJECTION

As we have seen, embodying either the darkest or the most idealised projections of other people can be problematic, particularly for those in positions of authority. There is a disconnect between the true self and the mask that is adopted or role that is assigned, where followers and detractors only see and latch onto a part of the whole.

Heifetz and Linsky argue that because leaders are subject to the projection of unrealistic expectations, it is inevitable that they will always disappoint their followers. The challenge they then face is to reveal glimpses of their real selves at a pace their followers can tolerate. This approach is analogous to how a parent gradually reveals more nuanced aspects of life as their children mature and become capable of grasping complexity.

In addition to these third-party projections and expectations, we also must learn to manage our first-person projections. In his poem *Song of Myself*, Walt Whitman famously declared, "I contain multitudes." We carry within us a host of archetypes and personas that are engaged in constant dialogue, often competing for their place on the stage, projecting negative and positive traits onto one another.

In *Your Symphony of Selves*, Fadiman and Gruber argue that each "has its own agenda, its own needs, and its own ways of working with your other selves and other people." Acts of imagination, internal conflict and dialogue all can heighten self-knowledge and personal awareness of both our strengths and limitations. However, we must exercise caution, as self-awareness can become a tool for spiritual bypassing. The more aware we become of our Shadows, the more adept we can become at hiding from them.

Certainly, the cacophony that emerges from our multiple selves makes us more conscious of our patterns of thought, our biases and how our emotions influence what we do. On occasion, what is projected onto one of these selves may become idealised, embodying a self-image we aspire to. We then are prompted to act on it and to constrain those other selves that may inhibit or block its realisation.

Former Olympian Victoria Pendleton has often referenced the importance of her relationship with psychiatrist Steve Peters during her career as a multi-medal-winning track cyclist. Peters, the author of *The Chimp Paradox*, always places great emphasis on visualisation, such as seeing a version of yourself crossing the finish line in first place or standing on the top step of the podium. In addition, he stresses the importance of emotional regulation, mental resilience and focus on performance.

Richard Linklater's 2023 film *Hit Man* examines these themes of identity and projection. The protagonist, Gary Johnson (Glen Powell), is a psychology lecturer who moonlights with the New Orleans Police Department in undercover sting operations. When forced to impersonate a contract killer, Gary discovers the power of inhabiting alternate identities. His alter ego, Ron, gradually becomes more than just a performance; he becomes a means of exploring and integrating his Shadow self.

The confidence, style of dress and demeanour Gary displays as Ron gradually transforms who he is. As he becomes more social and engaging, the change is noted by both his police department colleagues and college students. Through his burgeoning relationship with Madison (Adria Arjona), moreover, both characters break free from their initial limitations, finding empowerment through role-playing and embracing previously suppressed aspects of themselves. The film poses a Winnicottian question: *When does a false self become a true self?*

While we usually view projection as a psychological defence mechanism, it can be far more than that. By stepping back and examining our responses, we can gain broader systemic insights. The labels we attach to others often reveal more about our own context – our political views, upbringing and introjected beliefs – than about the individuals themselves.

The most transformative approach is to identify and acknowledge shared values and aspirations, even when we seek to realise them through different paths. Projection, when approached with empathy and self-awareness, can be a powerful tool for personal growth and mutual understanding.

Ultimately, our multiple selves are not fragments to be feared or suppressed, but a rich, dynamic ecosystem to be understood, respected and occasionally, as in *Hit Man*, playfully explored. Used well, projection can leave us more whole, compassionate and empathic in our relationships with others.

Shadow Work teaches us the need to remain open rather than defensive, although, as we will explore in the following chapters, there are many more defensive tendencies that we must navigate.

SHADOW REFLECTIONS

- What qualities do you most admire or dislike in others, and how might these reveal something about your own unacknowledged gifts and Shadows?

- Recall a time when you felt you acted 'monstrously.' What internal or external pressures drove this behaviour, and what can you understand about yourself through this reflection?

- Describe something you have desired primarily because others desired it. How did it make you feel, both during the pursuit and after obtaining whatever it was you wished for?

- Have you ever witnessed someone being unfairly blamed or marginalised? What motivated you to speak up, or prevented you from doing so, and what does this reveal about your own relationship with conflict and justice?

- Reflect on projections others have made about you, both positive and negative. How do these say more about the person projecting than about you?

- Have you either idealised or demonised someone else? Can you recognise the complexity and humanity in these individuals beyond your initial perception?

- When you have been involved in a challenging interpersonal or group situation, how have you moved beyond individual blame to understand the multiple factors that contributed to it?

- How do the Shadow aspects you have identified offer opportunities for growth, compassion and a more nuanced understanding of yourself and others?

CHAPTER 3

DEFENCES

I will only cooperate with you as long as it serves me. Beyond that, there can only be rivalry or indifference.

Hernan Diaz
Trust

**It took you years to cross
The lines of self-defence.**

Leonard Cohen
The Letters

What defence mechanisms do we rely on to cope with our conflicted feelings and impulses? How do these defences protect us, and at what cost? What happens when our Shadows trigger protective mechanisms that prevent our growth and healing, or impact our relationships with others?

My own journey of understanding began when I coached a leadership group that practised deep psychological reflection. I was new to this work, eager to prove myself and hungry for validation. During one session, a staff member suggested that the positive feedback I had received might be due to my collusion with the group I was facilitating. They implied that I was not challenging participants enough.

In that moment, my defences flared. I felt attacked, misunderstood. Tears welled up, and I found myself trapped in a victim–persecutor situation that spiralled quickly beyond my control. The energy was charged, and I adopted a defensive and reactive position. It was only later that I learned that curiosity would have provided me with a different approach that was much more rewarding and powerful.

Instead of being defensive, what if I had asked myself, "Could I be colluding? What might I be protecting?" This simple shift from reaction to reflection could have transformed a moment of conflict into an opportunity for growth. Now, when I am challenged or feel defensive, I have learned to pause and ask myself, "What am I truly protecting here?"

Our defence mechanisms are far more complex than we realise. They manifest in ways both obvious and subtle, in the form of projection, scapegoating, cancel culture, competition and other ways that disguise our past traumas and repressed emotions. We create elaborate psychological barriers to avoid confronting the parts of ourselves we find uncomfortable or threatening.

The anti-immigrant unrest that erupted across the U.K. in August 2024, following a mass-stabbing incident, illustrated how psychological defences can fracture entire societies. This breakdown of social cohesion reflects a broader trend documented by the Pew Research Center, with political polarisation having reached unprecedented levels. In the United States, the middle ground has virtually disappeared, with political camps moving to increasingly extreme positions. Misinformation, social media and partisan rhetoric frequently transform tragic events into explosive situations, with each side seeing only darkness in the other, unable to acknowledge complexity or shared humanity.

Organisations like More in Common have been documenting this alarming breakdown of collaboration, revealing how we've lost the ability to see our shared values. It is as if we have developed spiritual myopia, unable to see depth, nuance or the possibility of multiple truths existing simultaneously. We cluster with those who look, sound and think like us, creating echo chambers that reinforce our existing beliefs and shut out alternative perspectives.

For leaders, the real work lies in creating psychological safety that allows people to lower their defences. This requires a deep understanding of how our own unconscious mechanisms can sabotage genuine connection and learning. As leaders, we must be able to recognise our own defensive patterns, which protect us from vulnerability but prevent us from engaging meaningfully with others. These operate not just at an individual level, but can become institutionalised, affecting entire organisations.

Psychoanalyst Isabel Menzies Lyth's work on social defence systems helps illustrate how organisations systematically protect themselves from the uncertainty that accompanies change. These defences often create Shadow systems, those unofficial ways of coping with what the formal system cannot address. For instance, the U.K.'s National Health Service has deployed technological solutions, like electronic health records and AI-powered triage, to protect staff from the emotional burden and anxiety of directly confronting patients' suffering, unmet needs and frustrated expectations in an under-resourced system. While intended to manage the NHS's operational challenges, these systems have led to workarounds and informal processes that operate outside official procedures. Similarly, the outsourcing of certain services to private providers has introduced another layer of separation from the core public healthcare system. Large organisations like the NHS increasingly employ technological fixes to shield themselves from the very human needs they are meant to serve.

These organisational defence mechanisms manifest in a variety of ways. For example, employees can become trapped in unproductive cycles, forming subgroups that either see themselves as superior or protect themselves against perceived threats. But leaders who can interrupt these patterns create space for more authentic dialogue. This means learning to notice when groups are operating from a place of fear rather than collaboration, seeking simplified solutions, or looking for direction from a 'saviour' figure rather than doing the complex work of genuine problem-solving themselves.

The most transformative leadership happens when we can distinguish between surface-level reactions and deeper underlying needs. This requires a willingness to slow down and ask curious questions rather than rushing to judgement. When we encounter resistance or defensiveness in our teams, the instinct is often to push harder, to overcome or dismiss. But true leadership invites exploration. It creates a container where people feel safe enough to examine their own defensive patterns.

The journey from defensiveness to discovery is not about eliminating our Shadows, but developing the courage to illuminate them. It requires self-awareness, compassion and curiosity, as well as a willingness to sit with discomfort. Our defences were formed to protect us. They have a positive intent, even if the outcome can, at times, be suboptimal. We learn and grow when we can look at our Shadows not as enemies to be fought, but parts of ourselves waiting to be understood and integrated.

CONFLICT

Imagine two neighbours locked in a long-standing dispute over a property line. On the surface, it appears to be a simple boundary issue, but beneath lies a complex web of unmet needs, personal histories and emotional triggers. The situation illustrates a fundamental truth about conflict, revealing that it is rarely about the surface-level disagreement. We are generally not in conflict about the thing itself, but the deeper unexpressed needs.

Conflict often stems from our deepest human desires for recognition, security and respect. Whether in a workplace rivalry, political election or community dispute, people are fundamentally driven by similar needs. The problem emerges when we draw hard lines between *us and them*, creating rigid beliefs that make compromise seem impossible.

A workplace scenario where two employees are constantly at odds provides an illustrative example. Fatima is a manager at a pharmaceutical company in Ontario. She believes that one of her team members, Ralph, is trying to undermine her, repeatedly sending project updates to her boss without consulting her and questioning her strategic decisions during team meetings. Meanwhile, Ralph feels Fatima is blocking his professional growth by consistently assigning him routine lab work while giving breakthrough research projects to others. From the outside, their conflict might seem petty. But a deeper exploration reveals that Fatima fears losing her position to a younger colleague, noticing how Ralph's prestigious PhD and cutting-edge research expertise draw admiring attention from senior leadership. Ralph, in turn, feels his innovative ideas are being ignored, including his proposal for a new clinical trial methodology that Fatima dismissed without proper consideration because of protocol constraints. Their apparent competition masks deeper insecurities and unmet needs for professional validation.

What is missing in the interaction between Fatima and Ralph is a willingness to step back from their defensive positions and truly understand each other's perspectives. The real leadership challenge is creating spaces where these underlying needs can be explored without judgement. This does not mean agreeing with everything, but instead developing the capacity to truly listen. By understanding the other person's perspective, we broaden our own worldview. Our fundamental beliefs might not change, but we become more accepting of complexity and enriched by the other person's perspective. In his book *Think Again*, organisational psychologist Adam Grant invites us to approach conversations with humility and openness. We should not seek to be 'right,' advocating and proving our point. Instead, we should be curious and willing to learn.

In most situations, conflict should not be eliminated but used as a catalyst for personal and collective growth. Think of conflict like a compost heap in a garden. What seems like waste – our disagreements, tensions and misunderstandings – can become rich soil for understanding and change. This approach draws inspiration from Eastern philosophical traditions, which have long recognised the value of holding seemingly contradictory ideas simultaneously.

This is like the way a skilled aikido martial artist uses an opponent's energy to deflect a blow rather than meeting force with more force. Instead of trying to defeat the other person, we learn to work with the energy of the conflict. Our minds often want to categorise experiences into neat, separate boxes. We prefer clear distinctions like right or wrong, good or bad. But reality is far more nuanced. The most profound insights often emerge when we are willing to sit with uncertainty and complexity.

When we are caught up in a disagreement with a partner, friend or colleague, often our first instinct is to defend our position. But what if we approached the conflict with curiosity, instead?

What if we asked, "What am I not understanding about your perspective?" It takes courage to admit 'I may be wrong.' Breaking the desire to respond immediately, by even a brief pause, can allow us to respond creatively.

In his book *Making Change that Lasts*, physician and broadcaster Rangan Chatterjee argues that our tendency to take offence impacts our well-being. He observes that nothing is inherently offensive. If it were, we would all be uniformly offended by the same things. Instead, our reactions stem from our individual nervous systems and interpretations. This is particularly relevant in today's cultural landscape, where a readiness to take offence has become almost reflexive, often leading to the immediate rejection of challenging ideas or perspectives. Knee-jerk responses can prevent us from engaging with potentially valuable insights about ourselves and others. When we automatically blame other people for our emotional responses, we surrender our agency, sometimes even to anonymous voices on social media. Instead of either immediately accepting or rejecting challenging perspectives, we can benefit from thoughtful examination of our reactions. While uncomfortable, this often leads to meaningful personal growth and deeper understanding.

Several practical frameworks can help navigate conflict more skilfully. The Nonviolent Communication conflict resolution process, developed by psychologist and mediator Marshall Rosenberg, focuses on identifying and expressing underlying needs without blame or judgement. This involves paying attention to how we use language to blame rather than to open dialogue. Instead of saying, "You never listen," we might say, "I'm frustrated because I need to feel heard." This approach can transform everyday conflicts. For instance, when a flatmate leaves dishes in the sink, instead of saying, "You're so inconsiderate, you always leave your dishes here," we might say, "When I see dishes left overnight, I feel frustrated because I need a clean space to cook in the morning."

The theory of Transactional Analysis, developed by psychologist Eric Berne, also alludes to family interactions. It suggests that communication generally happens from three psychological positions: those of the Parent, Child and Adult. For Berne, most conflict is derived from mismatches between these positions. Parent-to-Child communication, for example, contributes to Shadow formation and the development of the inner critic. The most productive interactions occur when we communicate on an Adult-to-Adult basis. In such scenarios, we engage rationally, without emotional manipulation or submission.

The same situation might prompt very different reactions from each of these positions. For instance, when faced with a missed deadline, someone in a Parent position might say, 'You should know better than this, I'm very disappointed in you,' thereby triggering shame. Someone in a Child position might respond, 'It's not fair, you're always picking on me,' signalling their defensive and emotional attitude. In Adult-to-Adult communication, however, a more rational and constructive response might be, 'I see that the deadline was missed. What happened, and how can we prevent this in the future?'

The key in all these approaches is the same. We need to move from a position of defensiveness to one of curiosity and understanding. It's not about being right but about connecting and finding common ground.

Conflict is inevitable, but suffering is optional. By developing our capacity to listen deeply, acknowledge different perspectives and work with, rather than against, the energy of disagreement, we can transform conflicts into opportunities for growth, understanding and connection.

SURFACE TENSIONS

The surface tensions between Fatima and Ralph mask deeper psychological wounds and organisational patterns that reveal critical insights into interpersonal and professional relationships. Their workplace conflict emerges as a complex interplay of suppressed emotions, unacknowledged insecurities and defensive mechanisms.

Superficially, their interactions are characterised by emotional detachment and an inability to communicate effectively. Their professional relationship becomes a battlefield of unspoken resentments and defensive strategies. Fatima carefully cultivates a persona of competence and control, while Ralph adopts a stance of passive resistance, each protecting themselves from perceived vulnerabilities.

Their interactions reveal a stark contrast between their external professional personas and their internal emotional landscapes. In team meetings and formal interactions, both maintain a veneer of professional courtesy, carefully suppressing their authentic feelings and adapting their behaviours to organisational expectations. This emotional suppression becomes a survival strategy, allowing them to navigate workplace tensions while concealing their deeper insecurities.

Beneath the surface, Fatima greatly fears professional obsolescence. Her aggressive management style and resistance to Ralph's ideas stem from an unconscious dread of being replaced by younger, more innovative colleagues. Conversely, Ralph sees his contributions as undervalued, his innovative thinking consistently marginalised by what he perceives as an entrenched and dismissive organisational culture.

In his book *Covert Processes at Work*, organisation and change leadership specialist Robert Marshak asserts that discrepancies between surface perceptions and what is hidden are typical of how most groups function. These covert processes, including personal agendas and unspoken cultural norms, often carry more weight in interactions than formal policies and procedures.

The unresolved tensions between Fatima and Ralph create an atmosphere of underlying paranoia and unease. Their workplace becomes a space of constant psychological manoeuvring, where each interaction is laden with unspoken competitive energy. This perpetuates a cycle of miscommunication and mutual misunderstanding, with neither party willing to address the root of their conflict.

As Marshak's research suggests, leadership effectiveness depends on recognising these covert processes and hidden dynamics, shedding light on what is in the Shadows and then working constructively with it. Without intervention, however, systemic interpersonal tensions can lead to organisational dysfunction, stifling innovation, collaboration and individual potential. At its worst, this can result in organisational collapse, as with the demise of Theranos, where covert processes thwarted direct challenge of the leadership team and its public pronouncements regarding what the company's blood testing technology could deliver.

In such environments of entrenched defensiveness, the burden of surfacing critical truths often falls to those willing to risk their careers and reputations by speaking out. This makes the role of whistleblowers both essential and precarious in organisational life.

WHISTLEBLOWER

A pattern of organisational defensiveness was powerfully spotlighted by several Theranos whistleblowers, including lab associate Erika Cheung and research engineer Tyler Schultz. After attempting to address their concerns through internal channels, including direct appeals to company president and chief operating officer Ramesh Balwani and board member George Schultz, they turned to outside help. Their eventual disclosures to the Centers for Medicare & Medicaid Services (CMS) and *Wall Street Journal* reporter John Carreyrou were crucial in exposing the company's systematic deceptions.

During her trial, Elizabeth Holmes later acknowledged and corroborated the issues raised by whistleblowers relating to technology and service quality. She claimed that they represented a missed opportunity for learning and improvement. Nevertheless, Theranos's initial responses to Cheung's and Schultz's internal appeals and external whistleblowing were like the way antibodies defend against a virus.

This is not an uncommon pattern in whistleblowing cases. Leadership coach Simon Western was a whistleblower in the U.K. health sector. When we discussed his experiences, he framed the role as standing up to the Shadow behaviours within an organisation. However, he discovered that, as the organisation is then mobilised to protect itself and prevent the dissemination of harmful information, the whistleblower begins to feel targeted and ostracised, with the full weight of the system directed against them.

This is a trait also identified by organisational theorist Kate Kenny in her book-length study *Whistleblowing: Toward a New Theory*. As she notes, "People who speak truth and are identified as whistleblowers find themselves excluded both within and outside the organisation." Despite their ethical stance and motivation to expose the truth for the public good, their vilification and stigmatisation is commonplace. In fact, it is far more surprising when the challenges posed by whistleblowers are embraced by an organisation's leadership and employees, and then used to enhance existing systems and processes.

The hostile treatment of whistleblowers has been an area of academic interest for attorney Mark Stein, who in *The Lost Good Self* builds on the ideas he and organisational behaviour professor Gianpiero Petriglieri introduced regarding projective identification. Stein argues that in situations where whistleblowers are stigmatised and rejected, their colleagues have gone through an unconscious process of splitting the good and bad aspects of their personalities and projecting the former onto the whistleblower. Recognition of their own 'lost' good selves induces shame and guilt, which triggers a defensive reaction. This results in rejection, anger, hatred and other irrational behaviour directed at the whistleblower.

Stein notes that these situations are highly charged because those who recognise in the whistleblower what they have lost are forced to confront their own shortcomings. At best, this can be a failure to address organisational deficiencies or malpractice. At worst, it is indicative of their own collusion. Not only do whistleblowers force them to see what is wrong, but alert them to their own role in creating this situation. They feel compelled, therefore, to defend against the whistleblower and the consequences of their actions.

This is probably why Cheung and Schultz felt they had no option but to leave Theranos and go public with their concerns, after having been so effectively shut down by senior executives and board members. What was worse in Schultz's case was that it was his own grandfather, former U.S. Secretary of State, Treasury Secretary and Secretary of Labor George Schultz, who refused to believe him when he raised the alarm, damaging their relationship.

INNER CRITIC

As with the Theranos case, in the television series *Succession*, the theme of whistleblowing is closely tied to the exploration of corporate misconduct, loyalty and power struggles. Under the patriarchal rule of Logan Roy (Brian Cox), each of the principal characters finds themselves caught between protecting the Logan family and its company, doing what they believe is morally right and pursuing whatever best serves their own interests.

For Kendall Roy (Jeremy Strong) that means blowing the whistle on his own father, whom he accuses of being complicit in the commission and cover-up of illegal practices. Kendall's actions represent just one of the ways he and his siblings, particularly Roman (Kieran Culkin) and Shiv (Sarah Snook), defend against the Shadows, frequently succumbing to inner criticism and self-sabotage even as they lash out at others.

Throughout the four seasons of *Succession*, Kendall, Roman and Shiv find themselves feeding their respective demons as they both indulge and defend against their own immorality, addictions and destructive tendencies. Whether through substance abuse and impulsivity (Kendall), acerbic humour and sexually inappropriate conduct (Roman), self-destructive personal relationships and the pursuit of power as a means of self-validation (Shiv), or the projection of their flaws on to others (all three), each of the siblings struggles with their darker impulses, seeking to avoid direct confrontation with the Shadow aspects of their personalities.

Yet, their father's forceful personality means that there is ultimately no escape from this confrontation. Logan's severe and judgemental persona becomes internalised by his children, serving as a critical inner voice even after his death. This is consistent with psychoanalyst Melanie Klein's work on the development of the superego. Klein maintained that this part of the psyche, which is responsible for self-criticism and moral judgement, forms during a child's early development. Exposure to parental and societal expectations can result in the formation of a harsh and punitive inner voice. For the Roys, this exposure persists long into adulthood, with the siblings infantilised despite the prestige attached to the family name.

Cognitive behavioural therapists often refer to the inner critic as a judge or saboteur. It contributes to the negative thought patterns, emotional distress and maladaptive behaviours we see manifested in each of the Roy children, including their elder half-brother Connor (Alan Ruck). It distorts their perception of reality and leaves them clinging onto irrational beliefs.

The Roy siblings deny their problematic behaviours, rationalise their poor decisions and regress after temporary signs of emotional development and self-improvement. Influenced by their inner critic, they repeatedly overcompensate, make grand gestures, seek external approval, and then sabotage their own actions, punishing themselves before others can do so.

The inner critic is a universal experience, an internalised voice of fear and judgement that haunts many individuals. Its origins lie in early experiences, often comprising internalised criticisms from parents, caregivers, teachers and society. In recent times, these have been amplified by social media's relentless commentary on body image, status, attitude and behaviour. When severe, this internal dialogue can be debilitatingly destructive, preventing personal growth and career advancement. In extreme cases, it can result in people taking their own lives.

Addressing the inner critic requires compassionate self-aware-ness. By recognising that these judgmental voices are not truly our own, we can begin to create distance from their harmful narratives. Techniques such as personifying the critic – for example, giving it a caricatured identity, like 'Salty Sally'

– can help diminish its power. The key is not to fight or judge the inner critic, but to acknowledge it with kindness and try to understand its original protective intent.

Healing involves reconnecting with our inner child, that vulnerable self who first absorbed these critical messages. Offering loving, supportive messages to ourselves, we can start to counteract years of internalised criticism. This practice of self-compassion transforms the inner critic from a harsh judge to a gentle, supportive presence.

DARK TRIAD

In *Succession*, the emotional instability of the Roy siblings stands in stark contrast to the imperviousness and ruthlessness of their father. Kendall, for example, embodies the emotional turmoil, anxiety, victim mentality and need for approval of an anxious narcissist. However unwittingly, he constantly shows his vulnerability. He lacks self-worth and a stable sense of identity and struggles to maintain healthy relationships with other people.

Logan, by contrast, like many people at the top of the corporate ladder, is a sociopath. He epitomises the manipulativeness, callousness and self-serving behavioural characteristics associated with the psychological concept of the Dark Triad. This comprises three closely related personality traits: grandiose narcissism, Machiavellianism and psychopathy. Each can serve as a defence mechanism against Shadow effects.

Grandiose narcissists often have a strong need to maintain their self-image and protect their ego. They project an inflated sense of self and seek to devalue others. Machiavellian people also are cunning, manipulative and exploitative in their pursuit of personal gain and their interaction with others. Psychopaths display a lack of empathy, emotional attachment or remorse in their dealings with other people.

The Dark Triad cocktail of traits enables such individuals to control and manage rather than confront and integrate the negative aspects of their own personalities. Their approach is maladaptive, resulting in interpersonal difficulties, emotional disconnection and a lack of personal growth and self-awareness. They show no capacity for the self-reflection and introspection necessary to acknowledge and work with their Shadows.

In the case of the fictional character Logan Roy – loosely modelled on several media moguls, including Rupert Murdoch and Robert Maxwell – we witness his preoccupation with exercising control over his family and ensuring his legacy. Logan frays the bonds he has with all his relatives, as well as with many of his closest business advisers. He has a total disregard for the needs of others, bending them to his will and taking macabre delight in playing his children off one another. With a strong sense of entitlement, he has little regard for ethical concerns or social norms.

Logan acts ruthlessly, and frequently in anger, with his own self-interest the only motivating factor. If it is to his benefit, then he has no qualms about doing harm and exploiting other people's weakness, regardless of whether they are friend or foe. It is his unprincipled and self-centred approach to business and life that informs the dysfunction of his family and the power struggles that surround his business.

GASLIGHTING, BULLSHIT AND LIES

Logan's modus operandi is deceptive and highly manipulative, employing a variety of techniques. To provide himself with more control over the narrative surrounding his family and company, he withholds information, denies facts, distorts the truth and gaslights others, especially his children, making them doubt their own grasp of reality, memory and judgement. Not only do such actions involve a breach of trust, they result in an imbalance of power, with Logan undermining other people's ability to gain knowledge and forcing them to question their own cognitive abilities.

Logan clings to the image of himself as commanding, decisive and strong. Because of this, he relies on these deceptive and manipulative techniques as defences, avoiding self-reflection and the anxiety and discomfort that is experienced when the Shadows are brought to the surface. By refusing to acknowledge their existence, he maintains his sense of control and avoids the difficult Shadow Work of self-acceptance and integration. Instead, he indulges in immoral tendencies with no regard for the consequences.

When it suits him, Logan falls into the category of *bullshitter*, as defined by philosopher Harry Frankfurt in his essay *On Bullshit*. For Frankfurt, while a liar knows the truth and deliberately says something false, a bullshitter does not care whether what they say is inherently true or false. Their intention is to impress or persuade, regardless of truth. They are indifferent to it and to the harm their proclamations can do to others. Logan switches at will from lying to bullshitting to gaslighting. All he is concerned with is himself and his own opinions.

Psychologist Ramani Durvasula, a specialist in narcissistic personality disorder, argues that gaslighting is one of the most insidious forms of psychological manipulation. In her book

It's Not You, she describes it as a gradual, calculated process where the manipulator systematically seeds doubt, persistently defending their distorted version of reality while deflecting any contradictory evidence.

The scale of such manipulation can be both intimate and massive. Donald Trump's repeated assertions of 'fake news' provide a chilling example of gaslighting on a societal level, where constant repetition of lies and attacks on credibility can warp collective perception. Historian Alexei Yurchak explores a similar phenomenon in his work *Everything Was Forever, Until It Was No More*, introducing the concept of *hypernormalisation*. During the post-Stalin, pre-Perestroika Soviet era, an entire population accepted an officially sanctioned version of truth that fundamentally contradicted their daily experiences.

The notion of imposed narrative is not confined to political systems. The business world offers equally compelling examples, such as the Wirecard AG accounting scandal. Between 2015 and 2019, *Financial Times* investigations revealed systematic financial fraud by the company's executives. Throughout this period, the German payment processor's leadership employed classic gaslighting tactics, dismissing credible fraud reports as fake news and portraying themselves as victims of a conspiracy. By aggressively deflecting scrutiny, they managed to continue fabricating transactions and partnerships until their eventual collapse in 2020, which exposed €1.9 billion in non-existent cash and led to the arrest of CEO Markus Braun and the flight of the COO Jan Marsalek, who remains a fugitive.

The motivations behind deception are complex and not always malevolent. In *Everybody Lies*, data scientist Seth Stephens-Davidowitz argues that human beings are rarely fully honest, especially regarding sensitive or stigmatised topics. Our lies often serve as masks, concealing our true selves while protecting our vulnerabilities.

Organisational psychologist Tomas Chamorro-Premuzic suggested to me that lies reveal something deeper about human nature – they provide traces of our Shadow selves. This perspective is echoed by spiritual traditions, particularly in Buddhist thought. Tibetan Buddhism teacher James Low, in *Finding Freedom*, introduces meditation practices that encourage individuals to witness their own self-deception, transforming inner observation into a path of personal honesty and growth.

In the workplace, these psychological dynamics can create toxic environments. Social psychology professor Tessa West's *Jerks at Work* provides a practical framework for understanding and navigating such challenges. She identifies difficult personality archetypes – from gaslighters to narcissists to credit-stealing colleagues – and offers strategies for survival and self-preservation.

I have been through this firsthand. In one role, I worked under a narcissistic boss. My most effective strategy for dealing with the situation was to find an ally who could validate my experiences. When faced with a passive-aggressive micromanager in another position, I learned that the best approach for me was a carefully negotiated departure. Rather than confronting the manager directly, I crafted a departure that maintained my professional dignity while protecting my mental well-being. By keeping the manager's ego intact and presenting a path forward that seemed beneficial to both of us, I was able to negotiate a favourable exit package.

Over the years, I have learned that it is important to document difficult interactions, seek support, recognise manipulation and be prepared to prioritise your own psychological health. While confrontation is not always advisable, especially with individuals lacking empathy, strategic disengagement can be the most powerful response. Sometimes, the most courageous act is knowing when to leave a harmful situation, preserving not just your professional reputation, but your sense of self as well. This is part of gaining understanding of our whole selves.

PSYCHOLOGICAL SAFETY

How can self-reflective enquiry prove effective at an organisational scale? When we are involved in group interactions, we may be willing to share our strengths, but how do we also overcome the fear of exposing our weaknesses and limitations? How constructive and accommodating can we be in responding to the faults we find in other people, especially when we recognise our own shortcomings in them?

The work of professor David Burkus is largely focused on organisational behaviour and leadership, building on psychoanalyst Wilfred Bion's theories regarding psychological defences and *container–contained* relationships, where leaders, caregivers or therapists can hold and process what is unbearable for the individual. Both Bion and Burkus emphasise the importance of processing emotional experiences, fostering creativity and establishing environments where individuals can confront and integrate unconscious aspects of themselves for personal and organisational growth.

The notion of psychological safety, as developed by leadership professor Amy Edmondson, is central to Burkus's approach. Many people believe they need an environment where they can be their whole selves – where they feel accepted and respected, are able to speak up, and can question and challenge without the threat of reprisal. In healthy organisations, they suggest, it is incumbent on leaders (containers) to provide a safe space where employees (contained) can express their thoughts and emotions.

Returning to Fatima and Ralph, their poor relationship contributes to the absence of psychological safety in their workplace. Fatima, through her controlling behaviours and systematic suppression of alternative perspectives, unconsciously cultivates an environment where genuine vulnerability and collaborative learning become impossible. She creates barriers to open dialogue, making it difficult for team members like Ralph to express dissenting views or innovative ideas.

Ralph experiences this lack of psychological safety as a form of systematic marginalisation. His innovative ideas are consistently invalidated, leading him to develop protective mechanisms and passively resist Fatima's way of doing things. This mutual reinforcement of unsafe psychological spaces prevents either party from engaging in authentic professional discourse.

Where there are psychologically safe environments, they can provide a useful foundation for collective Shadow Work, enabling members of a group or organisation to identify certain defence mechanisms and harness them in constructive ways. By gaining awareness of their own Shadow tendencies and those of their peers, they are better equipped to own and integrate them rather than repress or project them, displaying their authentic selves to their colleagues.

For instance, by removing the fear of failure and encouraging interpersonal risk-taking, a psychologically safe environment can reduce anxiety and offer opportunities for learning. This is enabled by a collective willingness to provide, receive and act on constructive feedback. The tenets of nonviolent communication proposed by psychologist Marshall Rosenberg – empathy, honesty, personal responsibility, mutual respect – provide a useful framework. They help improve interpersonal relationships, reducing the combative nature of discussion and the *othering* of people who have different opinions.

For some, however, this approach is too idealistic, far removed from the reality of many organisations. Chamorro-Premuzic offers a more nuanced perspective in his *Forbes* article, "Should You Bring Your Whole Self to Work?" He notes that many productive work environments are psychologically and polit-ically volatile, with the dominant culture less concerned with personal purpose and fulfilment than business effectiveness. He proposes a more balanced approach that respects professional boundaries, maintains a degree of personal privacy and focuses on competence and performance rather than self-expression.

It is possible to be honest and straightforward in a way that benefits the organisation without revealing all of yourself. For example, over several decades, the Toyota Motor Company has nurtured and developed a corporate culture and management philosophy known as The Toyota Way. This is primarily focused on operational excellence and the quest for continuous improvement. At Toyota, a working environment has been established in which employees are encouraged to speak up, contribute to decision-making, identify and learn from errors, take risks and exercise autonomy.

With its Project Aristotle, a research initiative aimed at understanding what makes teams successful, Google has specifically highlighted the importance of psychological safety and the role it can play when employees are encouraged to share ideas and concerns they might otherwise withhold. Inspired by an Edmondson paper, project participants were encouraged to embrace ambiguity and uncertainty, face up to their blind spots through the giving and receipt of feedback, and gain understanding of different communication styles. With an emphasis on openness and authenticity, they found that psychologically safe environments could reduce fear and anxiety and enable learning and growth.

However, as Chamorro-Premuzic implies, too much focus on safety and an aversion to any form of conflict can contribute to an overly protective corporate culture. This denies opportunities for constructive discussion and creativity. Rather than defending against the Shadows, an environment that is too safe can add to them, resulting in more repression, antipathy, anxiety and resentment.

As ever, leaders need to seek equilibrium. As Simon Western notes in *The Politics of Dissonance*, they must find a way to "live with and face dissonance" so that it "becomes part of a whole, not something to be weaponised or repressed." This is the territory of *both/and* – of constructive discussion and the accommodation of multiple points of view – rather than the polarisation of *either/or*, with the division and separation of light and shadow.

The tension between safety and constructive conflict becomes especially apparent in whistleblowing scenarios, which typically emerge in cultures where truth-telling feels unsafe. While leaders are key to fostering psychological safety, they must also recognise how their organisational power can inadvertently silence others. As leadership advisors Megan Reitz and John Higgins suggest in *Speak Out, Listen Up*, even well-intentioned leaders may underestimate how their mere titles can intimidate and distance others from speaking openly.

Their TRUTH (Trust, Risk, Understanding, Titles, How-to) framework offers practical guidance for improving organisational dialogue. Leaders can create safer spaces through skilful questioning techniques, such as, "If there were to be a different perspective on this issue, what would it be?" The framework emphasises understanding organisational politics, acknowledging power relationships and developing awareness of how social hierarchies influence communication patterns.

The response to dissenting voices is particularly important. When group consensus appears too readily, it often signals an underlying lack of psychological safety rather than genuine agreement. Simple process adjustments, like allowing individual reflection time before team discussions, or the leader speaking last, can help prevent reactive responses and the usual voices dominating proceedings. Such practices help mitigate Shadow defences in organisational settings, creating environments where authentic dialogue can flourish.

POLITICAL CORRECTNESS

Organisations often struggle to balance meaningful change with defensive posturing, particularly when it comes to diversity, equity and inclusion (DEI) initiatives and environmental, social and governance (ESG) responsibilities. These workplace tensions surface daily through individual interactions and company policies.

Consider how Fatima and Ralph, like many professionals, must carefully navigate workplace dynamics. Fatima, a senior manager, uses precise language and formal communication as protective armour, maintaining professional distance while masking deeper complexities. Ralph responds with his own form of self-protection through strategic silence, recognising that speaking too freely could jeopardise his position. Their exchanges mirror countless similar scenarios playing out in offices around the world, where employees carefully modulate their authentic selves to fit institutional expectations.

However, when organisations push too hard on political correctness and compliance, it often backfires. In many workplaces, diversity initiatives face criticism when employees report feeling unable to openly discuss challenges without fear of repercussion, whether that relates to asking questions about implementation or raising concerns about effectiveness. Similarly, when companies adopt aggressive ESG targets, it can create a culture of silence around legitimate business concerns, with employees feeling pressured to prioritise compliance metrics over other important considerations. Rather than fostering genuine dialogue about discrimination or environmental impact, rigid compliance can turn meaningful initiatives into superficial checkbox exercises.

This superficiality invites valid criticism about corporate white-washing and greenwashing. Unilever, despite its reputation for sustainability leadership, faced scrutiny over labour practices in its developing-world supply chain. Volkswagen, after its emissions scandal, poured billions into electric vehicles and sustainability initiatives, yet questions remain about whether the company's underlying culture had truly changed. Other companies, like BP and Shell, have faced similar scepticism about their green initiatives as they continued significant fossil fuel operations.

The public's response to perceived corporate hypocrisy has intensified in the era of social media. What might once have been limited criticism can now escalate into full-blown cancellation campaigns, as companies like Anheuser-Busch InBev and Target discovered when their DEI initiatives sparked boycotts. While accountability is important, this polarised environment can hinder productive dialogue about complex social issues.

As explored by journalists Greg Lukianoff and Rikki Schlott in *The Canceling of the American Mind*, this culture of swift judgement and intolerance often leads to more separation than integration. This has manifested dramatically in cases like the Mozilla CEO who resigned over past political donations and the Google engineer fired for his memo about gender differences. These were cases where nuanced discussion gave way to immediate condemnation.

The result, as experienced during events like the U.K. riots, is that when dialogue breaks down, frustration can erupt into violence. Meanwhile, those targeted by public shaming campaigns face lasting personal and professional consequences that may far outweigh their perceived transgressions.

SHAME

Shame can lock parts of us away in the Shadows, especially when tied to trauma. When we feel intensely ashamed of experiences or aspects of our personality, we often defend against them through suppression and avoidance. Rather than acknowledging and integrating these elements into our conscious awareness, we compartmentalise them. This fragmentation, while seemingly protective, ultimately hinders our ability to heal and grow.

Guilt and shame, though often confused, operate at fundamentally different levels of human experience. Guilt arises from specific actions, which prompt the thought, *I did something bad*. It focuses on behaviour that, potentially, can be corrected or made right. Shame, by contrast, cuts deeper into our sense of self, manifesting as the belief, 'I am bad.' Rather than affecting our actions, this attacks our core identity. When shame originates from trauma, particularly early childhood experiences, it can be especially devastating because it may have taken root before the individual has developed the capacity for verbal expression or conscious memory.

In the case of Fatima and Ralph, instances of shame reveal deep psychological wounds that shape their professional interactions. Fatima's shame is rooted in her fear of professional irrelevance, which has become particularly acute given Ralph's academic qualifications and research expertise. It manifests as hyper-vigilance against perceived threats to her status, exemplified by her quick dismissal of Ralph's clinical trial methodology proposal. Her unconscious narrative – 'If I appear vulnerable, I will be replaced' – stems from early career experiences where she had to constantly prove herself in a male-dominated industry. This drives both her aggressive displays of competence and her systematic rejection of perspectives that challenge her established expertise. It is also visible in how she relegates Ralph to routine lab work while keeping breakthrough research under her direct control.

Fatima's defensive masquerade prevents genuine connection with others, reinforcing the very isolation she fears.

Ralph's shame emerges from a sense of invisibility, a pattern established in his childhood as a middle child often overshadowed by his siblings' achievements. This early experience of being overlooked manifests in his workplace behaviour, especially his tendency to bypass Fatima and send updates directly to senior leadership. It is a desperate bid for the recognition he craves. His shame surfaces through passive resistance, emotional withdrawal and the erection of psychological defences to protect his wounded professional identity. Rather than directly confronting Fatima about being relegated to routine lab work, he channels his frustration into questioning her decisions during team meetings, recreating a familiar family dynamic where his voice was often lost in the crowd. He experiences shame as the cumulative effect of marginalisation, with the paradoxical effect that he both desires recognition and fears rejection.

These individual experiences of shame mirror broader patterns in organisational behaviour, where personal and corporate identities often become dangerously intertwined. The television series *The Dropout* illustrates this through its exploration of Elizabeth Holmes's (Amanda Seyfried) leadership of Theranos, dramatising how early trauma can shape corporate culture. Holmes's response to sexual assault at Stanford University and her mother's advice to insulate the experience establishes a pattern of emotional suppression that later defines her leadership approach.

Shame's function is to silence and create self-separation. This manifests in Holmes's business practices through rigid compartmentalisation, enabling her to maintain unwavering confidence while suppressing evidence of Theranos's technological and operational failures. Her shame becomes both a driver of success and a mechanism for denying weakness.

The series depicts two distinct forms of shame in organisational contexts: the shame of hubris leading to moral transgression and the shame of inadequacy stemming from unrealised ambitions. Holmes exhibits unhealthy shame, characterised by destructive behaviours and denial. This contrasts sharply with the healthy shame displayed by whistleblowers Tyler Schultz (Dylan Minnette) and Erika Cheung (Camryn Mi-Young Kim), who transform their moral discomfort into corrective action. The distinction appears most stark when we consider the actions of scientist Ian Gibbons (Stephen Fry), whose debilitating shame leads to alcoholism and suicide.

Through both personal and organisational examples, we see how unprocessed shame creates cycles of defensive behaviour and ethical compromise. Yet the presence of healthy shame, exhibited by those who acknowledge and integrate their moral discomfort, suggests a path toward organisational integrity and genuine growth.

POSITIVE DEFENCES

Shadow defences typically emerge in childhood as protective mechanisms against emotional pain, trauma and perceived threats. These defences originally serve to help us cope with experiences we are not yet ready to confront directly, providing a sense of safety and psychological balance. In adulthood, though, these same protective patterns may now be limiting our growth and undermining our relationships.

Nevertheless, even as they potentially hold us back, these Shadow defences serve as valuable signals, alerting us to unresolved issues and unmet needs. We cannot indefinitely ignore what has been repressed. Instead, we must find ways to acknowledge these patterns, gain insight into their origins and discover paths to healing.

Family therapist Richard Schwartz argues that Shadow defences offer the potential for transformation, resulting in greater self-awareness and personal development. His book *No Bad Parts* addresses how his Internal Family Systems (IFS) model enables people to heal from trauma and restore their sense of wholeness. The IFS approach recognises various internal 'parts' that make up our psyche, from inner critics and perfectionists to vulnerable child-like parts that carry our wounds. By understanding and working with these different parts, particularly those carrying trauma, IFS has proven particularly valuable in treating war veterans with Post Traumatic Stress Disorder. In these cases, protective mechanisms that once helped soldiers survive combat can be transformed into sources of resilience and leadership in civilian life.

Schwartz suggests that defences are not pathological responses to the Shadows, but parts of our internal system that perform an important function. They should be treated with respect, compassion and curiosity rather than being repressed. For Schwartz, because they are trying to protect us, all parts have positive intentions, even those that initially appear destructive or problematic.

An inner critic, therefore, might have developed to protect us from failure by pushing us to excel, while a people-pleasing part might have emerged to keep us safe in relationships where authentic self-expression felt dangerous. Such protective mechanisms can be transformed into powerful creative and entrepreneurial forces. The singer Lady Gaga, for instance, has openly discussed transforming her defensive mechanisms around past trauma into creative expression and advocacy, while entrepreneur Sara Blakely has channelled her fear of failure into meticulous attention to detail that helped build Spanx into a billion-dollar company.

Schwartz's approach to IFS therapy focuses on the unburdening of the protective parts, releasing the extreme beliefs and emotions associated with them, and allowing them to take on a more flexible and harmonious role in the psyche. This transformation is evident in the example of athlete Marcus Trescothick, who channelled his experience of anxiety and depression from a career-ending crisis into pioneering mental health advocacy in professional cricket, helping destigmatise mental health issues in elite sports.

The so-called *tor-mentors* – parts of the psyche that torment us but fulfil a mentoring and protective role – become powerful allies as we journey toward wholeness and understanding. The goal of IFS is not to eliminate the tor-mentors but to provide them with a more supportive role within our internal system. Microsoft CEO Satya Nadella exemplifies this integration, having transformed his experience as a parent of a child with severe disabilities from a source of anxiety into an impetus to make technology more accessible and inclusive.

However, this process and quest for balance must be handled carefully. Overplayed strengths and Shadow parts that distort perception or exacerbate conflicts can soon become derailers, the subject of the next chapter.

SHADOW REFLECTIONS

- In situations of conflict, can you identify underlying transactional analysis patterns? What would constructive adult-to-adult communication look like?

- What barriers prevent you from truly hearing and understanding others during conflict?

- When you feel offended, do you understand why? Do you take the time to reflect on the other person's perspective and what might have informed it before responding? Or, do you react immediately and unthinkingly? How often do you misinterpret the other person's intentions?

- What messages does your inner critic communicate? Can you trace these to their origin (parent, teacher, societal narrative)? How might you develop a more compassionate dialogue with this critical voice?

- What concrete steps can you take to create an environment where people feel safe to speak up and share difficult truths?

- How do you typically react when challenged or criticised? What would a more constructive response entail?

- Reflect on experiences with manipulative behaviours. What did you learn about yourself, your boundaries and your support systems?

- Have you ever been complicit in spreading misinformation or engaging in dishonest communication? What motivated these actions?

- How has shame prevented you from being genuine? What would authentic self-expression look like?

- What healthy strategies have you developed to protect yourself? How do they differ from more destructive coping methods?

- How do your defence mechanisms both protect and limit you? What would personal growth look like if you could transform these patterns?

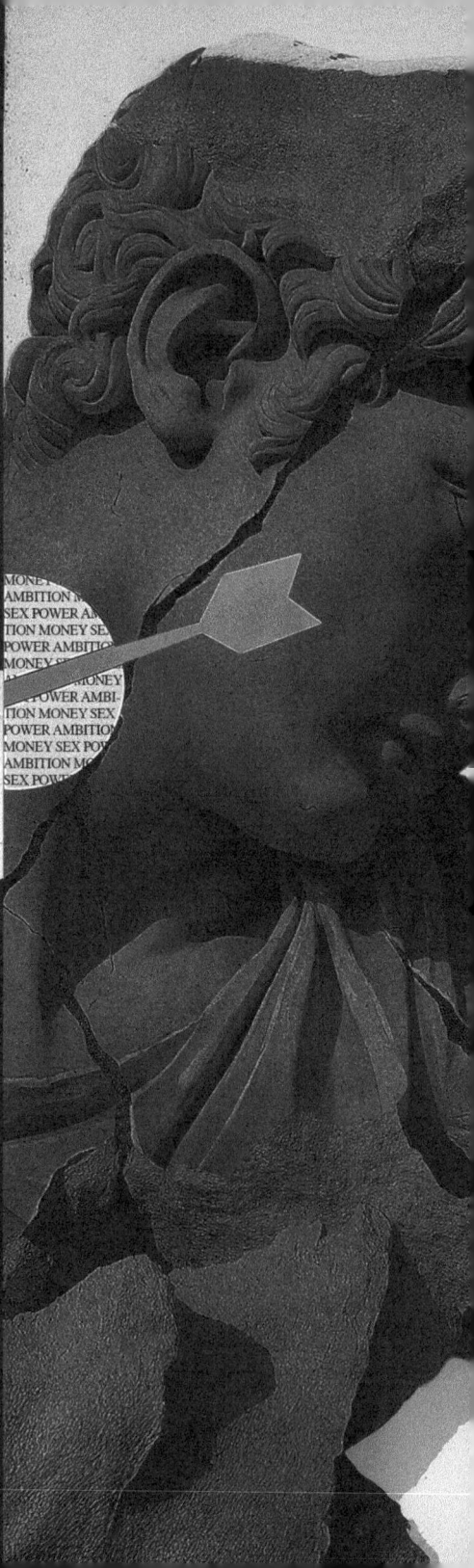

MONEY
AMBITION M
SEX POWER A
TION MONEY SE
POWER AMBITIO
MONEY S
POWER MONEY
TION MONEY SEX
POWER AMBITION
MONEY SEX POW
AMBITION MO
SEX POW

CHAPTER 4

DERAILERS

I frequently look back at my life, searching for that fork in the road, trying to figure out where, exactly, I went bad and became a thrill-seeking, pleasure-hungry sensualist, always looking to shock, amuse, terrify and manipulate, seeking to fill that empty spot in my soul with something new.

Anthony Bourdain
Kitchen Confidential

Always alert to the music of chaos. I've got a slightly sordid addiction to it.

Dana Czapnik
The Falconer

What are the hidden pitfalls that can derail not just individual leaders, but entire organisations and systems? How do our strengths, when overused or misapplied, become weaknesses that ripple through our teams and institutions? In what ways do our collective blind spots and unexamined assumptions create vulnerabilities that can cascade into systemic failures? What is the relationship between derailers and our Shadows? How can facing the darkness we hold inside help us navigate these potential obstacles?

Derailers can be understood as behaviours and personality traits that impair leadership effectiveness, but their impact extends far beyond individuals. As psychologist Robert Hogan argues, these dark-side tendencies are particularly dangerous because they often masquerade as strengths. A leader's decisiveness can manifest as reckless impulsivity under pressure, healthy scepticism can deteriorate into paranoid distrust, while appropriate caution can become paralysing risk aversion.

In *Twenty Years on the Dark Side*, Hogan and his co-authors maintain that "the problem with the dark-side tendencies is that they disrupt relationships and corrupt judgment, destroying trust and driving bad decision-making, which ultimately undermines leaders' credibility and impact." These effects multiply across organisational levels, creating ripple effects that can ultimately undermine entire systems.

Steinhoff International, for example, was once one of South Africa's largest retailers, operating popular chains like the Pep clothing and homeware stores across the country. What began in 2017 as the exposure of accounting irregularities stemmed from the leadership team's overconfidence. CEO Markus Jooste's aggressive pursuit of international expansion and unilateral decision-making exemplified this problem. The company's leaders compromised governance systems by manipulating financial statements and creating complex structures to hide losses.

This pattern of deception led to its liquidation in 2023. The collapse devastated not just shareholders, but also South Africa's financial sector and pension system, with the Government Employees Pension Fund suffering massive losses.

Like Shadows, derailers operate outside our conscious awareness, only gaining visibility when they cause problems or are pointed out by others. While they often emerge as overused strengths, they can also serve as defences protecting against vulnerability, sometimes becoming visible when we overcompensate for weaknesses. This plays out not just individually, but collectively. Teams can develop shared blind spots, while organisations can institutionalise defensive routines that protect against uncomfortable truths but ultimately undermine their effectiveness.

The systemic nature of derailers becomes evident when we examine how organisational failures cascade through interconnected systems. As sustainability expert Jem Blendell argues in *Breaking Together*, systemic collapse occurs not as a single event but as a process where the failure of one system accelerates the deterioration of others. We see this in cases like the 2018 collapse of multinational construction and facilities management company Carillion in the U.K., where the derailers of aggressive risk-taking and deliberate blindness to mounting debt triggered cascading failures affecting thousands of suppliers, employees and public service projects, eventually exposing deep flaws in the U.K.'s outsourcing model.

The likelihood of both individual and systemic derailment demands that we examine the potential for darkness in leadership at all levels. Yet, with some notable exceptions, there is an evident bias in contemporary business literature and training programmes toward the bright side. The promotion of positive psychology, psychological safety, appreciative inquiry and authenticity, among other trends, at times can overemphasise the positive aspects of leadership while leaving us blind to systemic risks.

Recent business history provides numerous examples of how individual and systemic derailers intertwine. At Abraaj Group, once the Middle East's largest private equity firm, founder Arif Naqvi's charismatic leadership style and ambitious vision initially resulted in remarkable success. However, these same qualities evolved into derailers when unchecked confidence led to misuse of investor funds and opacity in operations, ultimately causing the firm's collapse in 2018 and sending shockwaves through emerging-market investment.

At Brazil's mining company Vale, repeated warning signs about dam safety were ignored, including internal technical reports highlighting structural weaknesses and employee concerns about monitoring systems. These unheeded warnings led to the catastrophic Brumadinho disaster that claimed 270 lives. The tragedy forced Vale to transform its safety culture and governance, implement new risk management systems and establish an independent safety board.

Even successful leaders like Uday Kotak of India's Kotak Mahindra Bank have faced potential derailment. In his case, this was through initial resistance to regulatory pressure to reduce his stake in the bank, although he did eventually recognise the importance of compliance and effective succession planning.

The Vale and Kotak stories demonstrate how confronting Shadow aspects – whether in the form of organisational blindness to risk or personal attachment to control – can catalyse meaningful change. Vale's enhanced safety protocols and Kotak's embrace of governance reform shows how leaders can emerge stronger when they acknowledge and address their derailers.

For many, though, leadership derailers often have their roots in the very qualities that bring initial success, including overconfidence, perfectionism, impulsiveness, an inability to delegate and the avoidance of constructive conflict. These traits can become embedded in organisational culture, creating systemic vulnerabilities. Gender dynamics add another layer of complexity. The psychologist Tomas Chamorro-Premuzic notes, for example, how male overconfidence often masks competence gaps, while women face double binds where assertiveness is viewed as selfishness and vulnerability as weakness. These patterns become systemic barriers that limit organisational effectiveness and resilience.

When left unaddressed, derailers create dysfunction that spreads from individuals to teams to entire organisational systems. This raises critical questions for contemporary businesses: How can leaders identify potential derailers before they become problematic? What strategies can transform these liabilities into assets? How can organisations create cultures that recognise and constructively address risks at all levels? Perhaps most importantly, how can leaders recognise and intervene in cascading systemic failures before they pass critical tipping points?

It is inevitable that we all will derail at some point in our lives. This is part of being human and helps foster shared empathy. As Buddhist teacher Pema Chödrön reminds us, "Things fall apart." When we notice a leaking tap, we have a choice: We can address it willingly and fix it early, or we can wait until the flood comes and the ceiling collapses, forcing us, finally, to confront the issue. By facing our Shadows and working with them consciously while things are going well, we can reduce the likelihood of being dragged into a crisis in the future.

POWER

In his book *Power*, business theorist Jeffrey Pfeffer maintains that power is a crucial aspect of organisational life and individual success. He suggests that the ability to acquire and wield power is not innate, but must be learned and developed as we adapt to the politics and relational complexities of our organisations. His advocacy of power and its leverage, however, is not without its risks. There is a Shadow aspect to power that requires careful attention and management.

Understanding power relationships begins with self-reflection and mapping. Leaders must create visual maps of their connections and interactions, both within and outside their organisations. This exercise reveals the sources of emotional support, information, political influence and creative ideas. It raises important questions: From whom do we derive our power? Are we overly dependent on certain individuals? What would happen if we lost their support? Such mapping also highlights how power intersects with gender, diversity and identity, as well as how it shifts across different contexts and groups.

While most companies maintain hierarchical organisational charts, there often exists a Shadow organisation. This is an uncharted network through which people wield power and influence. They exercise this informal power by sharing or withholding knowledge, providing strategic assistance or building relationships across organisational silos. An executive assistant, for example, while not high in the formal hierarchy, derives significant power from controlling access to the CEO and connecting different parts of the organisation.

The pursuit of power, however, carries the inherent risk of corruption, especially when dark-side tendencies are not balanced by ethical behaviour. As political scientist Brian Klaas argues in *Corruptible*, we often witness a 'power paradox' where those most suited to positions of authority are least likely to seek them, while those least suited tend to obtain them and are soon derailed by the power they now hold. Even those who start out with good intentions can be corrupted by power, changing their behaviour, becoming more self-interested and less empathetic, while making increasingly poor decisions.

The scandal involving the Renault-Nissan-Mitsubishi Alliance's Carlos Ghosn illuminates how power can become a major leadership derailer and source of organisational dysfunction. Ghosn's story illustrates how power can amplify existing personality traits and lead to destructive behaviours. Reports of his arrogance, overconfidence, scepticism and paranoia are consistent with Hogan's exploration of the dark side of leadership. While such traits were relatively manageable early in Ghosn's career, they appear to have become more pronounced and problematic as he accumulated power and success.

Management consultant Kets de Vries's psychodynamic approach offers deeper insights into how power can corrupt, focusing on unconscious motivations, defence mechanisms and narcissistic leadership methods. In Ghosn's case, his Dark Triad tendencies were evident in the way he cultivated his public image, his willingness to act as if he were above the law, alleged use of corporate resources to fund his lavish lifestyle, imperviousness to criticism and reliance on fear to manage and control others. His ego was inflated by concurrent leadership positions across multiple organisations, leading him to abuse this accumulated power and exploit the structural complexities of the alliance between Renault, Nissan and Mitsubishi to his own ends.

The Ghosn case also illustrates what Chamorro-Premuzic identifies as a critical blind spot in leadership selection: the tendency for charisma and confidence to overshadow competence. Ghosn's *cultural intelligence* (CQ) in bridging French,

Japanese and global business norms initially obscured serious issues with his ethical decision-making. While his CQ helped build the automotive alliance, he ultimately exploited cultural differences in corporate governance to consolidate and misuse his power. This raises key questions about how we evaluate leadership potential in multinational contexts, particularly when cultural adeptness might mask darker tendencies.

Effective leadership requires the capacity to see and work with both codified power structures and Shadow dimensions. In *The Character of a Corporation*, the academics Rob Goffee and Gareth Jones identify four key organisational cultures – mercenary, networked, communal and fragmented – that reflect different forms of power relationships. A networked culture, for example, may foster collaboration but also lead to information overload and hidden conflicts because people are reluctant to disagree with one another and damage relationships.

As AI transforms traditional hierarchies, understanding these Shadow aspects of power becomes increasingly important. Shadow systems can disrupt and flatten our companies' structures, blurring traditional lines of authority. Leaders must be attuned to the informal networks, tacit knowledge and cultural influences that inform how power is wielded. Companies like W.L. Gore & Associates and engineering firm Semco exemplify how organisations can successfully integrate these invisible dimensions, allowing for greater autonomy, informal relationships and democratic decision-making in their operations.

Robert Chesnut, a former U.S. federal prosecutor who has held senior roles with eBay and Airbnb, highlights the importance of ethics and integrity in his book *Intentional Integrity*. He told me that leaders have a responsibility to set the tone for their organisations, however complex or multicultural they may be. Leaders must model the behaviour they expect of others, serving as thermostats rather than thermometers. They have a moral imperative to exercise their power and authority for the good of the company, its employees and other stakeholders, as well as its long-term future.

Exercising ethical leadership requires leaders to acknowledge both their own power and that of others, bringing Shadow dimensions into the light. As we gain organisational seniority, we must not be blind to the power we hold. Understanding power relationships and influence becomes a key skill regardless of our level or role. This awareness allows leaders to intentionally shape organisational culture to support their strategic aims, integrating the invisible with the visible, while remaining vigilant to power's potential as a derailer.

MONEY

Ghosn's story illustrates how the abuse of power often goes together with greed – the desire for not only organisational growth but also personal authority and the acquisition of wealth. It shows how the pursuit of money can also derail leadership, impairing decision-making, prompting unethical behaviour and encouraging unnecessary risk-taking. This is far from an exceptional case, as evidenced by financier Bernie Madoff's Ponzi scheme scandal, the subprime mortgage crisis that escalated into a global financial crisis and stockbroker Jordan Belfort's wolf-like activities on Wall Street.

Belfort founded the investment firm Stratton Oakmont in the 1990s. Whatever legitimate business aspirations he may have had were soon overwhelmed by a desire to make as much money as possible, to fuel the excessive lifestyle he and his colleagues enjoyed. Belfort showed a complete disregard for ethical business practices, accumulating personal wealth while manipulating stocks and defrauding investors. Greed would derail him and his business.

Stratton Oakmont operated a 'pump and dump' share scheme. The company would buy large quantities of penny stocks, which it then promoted aggressively to potential investors. Once the price became overinflated, Belfort and his colleagues would sell their shares, making a huge profit while leaving their unsuspecting investors with worthless stock. The company also engaged in securities fraud, making false statements about stocks it promoted and manipulating initial public offerings (IPOs) to the benefit of the firm and the detriment of the clients it represented.

Suspicious trading activity and whistleblower evidence ultimately proved to be Belfort's downfall. Stratton Oakmont was subject to investigations by the National Association of

Securities Dealers (NASD), the U.S. Securities and Exchange Commission (SEC) and the Federal Bureau of Investigation (FBI). It was eventually revealed that Belfort had been involved in money laundering to hide his illegal profits. This included using people to smuggle cash out of the U.S. and deposit it in Swiss bank accounts. Eventually, as part of a plea bargain, Belfort was sentenced to four years in prison and ordered to pay $110 million in restitution to the victims of his fraudulent activities.

The heady cocktail of money and power experienced by the likes of Ghosn and Belfort can cause leadership derailment even where criminality is not involved. Ethical considerations and concern for others are set aside when leaders become more self-centred and protectionist regarding their access to wealth and the exercise of power. This has become something of a dominant model under post-industrial capitalism. Fear of *the other*, of what lurks in the Shadows and poses a threat to the Establishment, is a motivating factor.

Such threats are often neutralised and absorbed. For example, start-up organisations and the entrepreneurs behind them often begin by challenging the Establishment, but eventually become key players in the business, economic and political mainstream. They transform into stalwart defenders of the status quo that concentrates wealth into 'the 1%,' protecting their own positions and financial interests. This is a recurrent pattern. What happened with the change-making captains of industry early in the 20th century has happened again in the 21st, involving the likes of Peter Thiel, Elon Musk, Jeff Bezos, Mark Zuckerberg and others.

Musk presents an intriguing example. The more power and wealth he has acquired, the more he projected a rightward shift toward individualism and libertarianism, eventually moving into alignment with various autocrats and extremist ideologies in his public statements and actions. This represents a dramatic break with his historic political affiliations and personal beliefs. Such discrepancies suggest that his accumulation of wealth, and desire to shield and grow it, has played a role in his decision-making. It has influenced how he leads, what he will permit on the platforms that he owns and how far he is willing to go to protect what he has.

In *Winners Take All*, journalist Anand Giridharadas argues that a similar protectionist undercurrent informs modern philanthropy and the role of the wealthy elite in addressing social problems. Under the influence of Establishment figures, there is a tendency to rely on business and market principles when tackling the need for societal reform. Rather than adopting a systemic perspective, this focuses on the individual and the retention of existing power structures. It fails to tackle the root causes of systemic inequality, poverty and other social ills, continuing to advantage the wealthy and enhancing their influence on public policy.

Here, the donation of money is designed to lock in the system that enabled the donors to amass their wealth in the first place. Yet again, the care, empathy and social conscience demanded of the modern leader is trumped by self-interest, with money derailing any possibility of leadership effectiveness. The access to money remains a means to suppress and control those who do not have it. Cryptocurrencies offer a telling contemporary example. While advocates tout the promise of financial independence and global mobility, these digital currencies also have enabled a Shadow economy where criminal networks can easily launder money and convert illicit gains into legitimate assets, such as luxury real estate. What is presented as financial democratisation can serve to reinforce existing power structures while creating new avenues for financial misconduct.

These systemic issues around money and power become deeply personal when we examine our own relationship with wealth and security. Our attitudes regarding money are largely unconscious, rooted in the circumstances into which we were born, what we experienced during childhood and the prevailing culture and social norms during both our early years and adulthood. My work provides a sufficient income, yet I still have an irrational fear of not having enough, losing what I have and experiencing poverty. Some of my fears are informed by my childhood, growing up on a council estate. We were never short of love, but both my parents had to work very hard, with my father taking on double shifts and night work to provide enough money to support three children.

Financial psychologist Brad Klontz has developed a theory of *money scripts*, which, like theatrical scripts used by actors, determine how we behave and act in relation to money. He argues that these scripts are unconscious, passed down and based on partial truths. Klontz identifies four distinct money belief patterns: money avoidance, money worship, money status and money vigilance. I can see that my own concerns and vigilance about money today are closely linked to my childhood family experiences.

To avoid money-related Shadows derailing us, we need to gain awareness of the money scripts that govern us. Conscious reflection on our money beliefs and frank conversations with those we love can help establish a healthier relationship with money and the role it plays in our lives.

TALENT

Many of the people we have encountered so far in this chapter attained leadership roles because of their talent, but were then derailed by their lust for power, greed or a combination of the two. However, through their groundbreaking research, INSEAD scholars Jennifer and Gianpiero Petriglieri have shed light on a largely hidden phenomenon: talent itself also can serve as a derailer. But given the sensitivity of the cases they have studied, as well as the scarcity of relevant stories that have not been anonymised, their ideas may be best illustrated here with a hypothetical example.

Shortly after graduating with a first-class degree, Ayanna was recruited by a prestigious investment bank. Her bosses soon took note of her incisive analytical skills and ability to identify lucrative opportunities. Ayanna moved rapidly up the corporate ladder, consistently outperforming her peers in terms of the deals she made and the level of client satisfaction she attained. Within two years of joining the bank, she was an associate, and within a few more she was a vice president.

But with the recognition and reward of her talent came immense pressure. Ayanna was expected to continue outperforming not only her colleagues but her own past successes. As her superiors sought to leverage her technical expertise, she was constantly assigned the most challenging clients and most complex deals. The bank's senior executives became over-reliant on her core strengths, while neglecting her development in other areas. Now responsible for many other people, she lacked communication, people management and leadership skills.

Having always been the star, with demonstrable knowledge and experience in a narrow field, Ayanna didn't know how to ask for help or admit to others that she was feeling overwhelmed by her additional responsibilities. As she tried to adapt to her new role, she became more conservative and risk-averse in the very areas of business where she had previously excelled. Unable to delegate or communicate clearly, she took on too much herself.

Under increasing stress, Ayanna lost focus when negotiating a new deal, leading to a series of poor decisions. Ultimately, this lost the bank a major client and the potential for significant future revenue. Everything she had feared while trying to live up to her 'talented' status had now come to pass, and her once stellar reputation was tarnished not only in her own eyes but in those of her superiors and colleagues. Ayanna's career subsequently stalled. Repeatedly passed over for promotion and stuck in a role she did not enjoy, she eventually resigned from the bank.

Ayanna's story illustrates what psychologist Carol Dweck describes as the shift from a growth mindset to a fixed mindset. Rather than continuing to learn and develop new skills, those characterised as talented often become fixed in their ways, taking fewer risks and focusing on protecting their status and the idealised perceptions other people have of them. This psychological response to the talent label is precisely what concerned the Petriglieris in their research.

In their *Harvard Business Review* article, 'The Talent Curse,' they highlight the need for a more holistic approach to talent management that considers long-term career development and personal well-being. While many organisations fast-track those they have identified as talented, this can be a double-edged sword. It can create unrealistic expectations too early in someone's career. The individual feels trapped, constantly under pressure to perform, inhibited by a fear of failure and stifled by a lack of growth opportunities that would enhance their knowledge, skills and capabilities.

As in Ayanna's example, this can result in stress, anxiety and burnout. The stars of the future suddenly find themselves derailed from their once-promising careers. They become risk averse and conformist, followers rather than leaders. They either become preservers of the status quo, stuck in middle management positions, or they become former employees seeking to reset their careers. They have been scuppered by their efforts to take on the unattainable mantle of the ideal executive.

When I spoke with Jennifer Petriglieri, she drew parallels between narcissism and the effects of being pegged as talented. "It's all Shadow and no self," she observed. In effect, talent becomes unmoored from the self, perceived superficially through the eye of the beholder rather than understood as an individual's inner quality. The talented label and the expectations that come with it are divorced from the individual's subjective experience. As with Winnicott's distinction between the *true self* and the *false self*, there is a disconnect between what once made these people stand out and what they feel they must now live up to.

"Our greatest talents often spring from wounds and quirks," the Petriglieris argue in their *HBR* article, "from the rougher, less conformist sides of ourselves." This relates to the concept of the Golden Shadow, those suppressed gifts and capabilities we have not yet claimed for ourselves but recognise in others. While overusing our established strengths can lead to derailment, sometimes the very qualities we previously viewed as negative can become valuable assets if we learn to harness them effectively. By accessing them, we move closer to unlocking our full potential.

In one workplace scenario that I witnessed, a team member who was initially viewed as overly critical and negative – qualities which are themselves potential derailers – was eventually recognised as the source of valuable contrarian perspectives that prevented groupthink. What initially appeared to be a liability became an asset when reframed and skilfully deployed. This helped me see how potential derailers can be transformed into valuable contributions when properly understood and managed.

"We sit looking in the lake, at the outer thing, at the reflection," Jennifer told me, developing her narcissist analogy. "And we end up drowning it." The key to avoiding this fate lies not just in managing our recognised talents, but in developing a growth mindset that allows us to explore and integrate our Shadows, including both the qualities we over-rely on and those we have yet to claim as strengths.

IDENTITY

Why do we often self-destruct or derail when everything seems to be going well? The answer is deeply rooted in our identity and self-narrative. As neuro-linguistic programming expert Robert Dilts's Logical Levels Model suggests, sustainable change requires transformation at the identity level. Otherwise, our behaviours will inevitably revert to align with our core self-concept.

Ayanna's story perfectly illustrates this connection between identity and behaviour. Despite her exceptional technical abilities and rapid rise through the ranks, her fundamental self-image remained that of a technical specialist rather than a leader. When faced with leadership responsibilities that challenged this identity, she retreated to her comfort zone and became increasingly risk averse. This mirrors what psychologist Gay Hendricks describes in *The Big Leap* as the upper limit problem, which is a form of self-sabotage that occurs when our success exceeds our internal self-concept.

Hendricks identifies four barriers that can trigger this identity-based derailment, and we can see several at play as Ayanna's story unfolds. Her intense fear of being found out suggests she was struggling with *feeling* fundamentally flawed, believing that she was not truly worthy of her senior position. Her reluctance to admit vulnerability or seek help also hints at a *fear of outshining* complex, having internalised messages about the dangers of overly standing out.

The power of these identity narratives becomes particularly evident in how Ayanna responded to pressure. Rather than seeing challenges as opportunities for growth, she interpreted them as threats to her identity as someone who was talented. This shift to a fixed mindset created a self-fulfilling prophecy, with her fear of failure realised because of her own behaviour.

Research by the Petriglieris and organisational behaviourist Herminia Ibarra reinforces this understanding, suggesting that successful transitions, particularly in leadership roles, require identity work, not just skill development. Sustainable success depends on our ability to revise our self-narrative to accommodate new roles and responsibilities. Without this identity-level change, even the most talented individuals may find themselves trapped in cycles of self-sabotage.

This has profound implications for personal development programmes. Just as a dieter who has not internalised the identity of a healthy person is likely to revert to old eating habits once their diet ends, professionals who have not integrated a new leadership identity into their self-concept may struggle to maintain new behaviours under pressure. To prevent derailment, we must work at both the behavioural and identity levels, examining and updating the deep-seated narratives that guide our actions.

COMPLEXES

The Petriglieris' thesis about the talent curse points to an interplay with psychological complexes, where this can exacerbate existing complexes or even result in the emergence of new ones. In Jungian terms, a complex can be understood as a group of related, unconscious ideas, feelings and impulses that influence our behaviour, attitudes and actions. Complexes tend to be emotionally charged, causing internal conflicts and maladaptive behaviours that often derail us.

In Ayanna's case, several complexes were in play, feeding off her experience of the talent curse and its effects. When pushed beyond her comfort zone and promoted to a position where she lacked the necessary competencies, Ayanna's imposter complex intensified her fear of being found out and exposed as a fraud. To deflect, she took on more work than she could handle, resulting in the critical oversights that lost the bank business.

At the same time, Ayanna's perfectionist complex prompted her to set impossibly high standards for herself, increasing the stress and anxiety she experienced. As she strived to maintain her flawless image, she became increasingly risk-averse, suppressing qualities that had led to her success. While she struggled to mask her growing insecurities, Ayanna also developed a superiority complex, projecting an air of infallibility. This prevented her from seeking guidance and support from others, which might have helped her develop the leadership and communication skills required to be effective in her VP role.

Perhaps most damagingly of all, the self-defeating beliefs and behaviours of the saboteur complex took hold. In a paradoxical response to the pressure she was under, Ayanna almost guaranteed that what she most feared would happen. She began to put off essential tasks and decisions, leaving them until the last minute. When, for the first time in her career, she started to forget important meetings and misplace key documents, Ayanna also began to pay more attention to her inner critic, which further undermined her self-confidence and ability to fulfil her duties to the highest standard.

For Ayanna, the pressure to always perform at an exceptional level fuelled her complexes, creating a vicious cycle that caused her derailment. These complexes, in combination with the talent curse, challenged how Ayanna saw herself, affecting her sense of identity and her worldview. This posed a threat to her ego, which is itself a complex that works hard to defend itself.

The organisational development consultant Laurence Barrett explained to me that the ego complex "has an energetic response to anything that challenges the hegemony of the rational." The ego can be extremely resistant to acknowledging our darker aspects, represented by the Shadows. From a Jungian perspective, this becomes a major hurdle to integration, development and growth, leaving issues unresolved and repressed in the unconscious.

Complexes have their own goals, values and trajectories that may not align with the intentions of the conscious ego. They are autonomous parts of the psyche. Complexes actively resist integration and exposure, hiding in the unconscious. And often, as in Ayanna's case, they can prompt compulsive and irrational behaviour. Even when we do develop awareness of a complex and attempt to consciously change our behaviour, the complex will test our resolve, creating internal conflict and adding to our sense of derailment.

The correlation between complexes and derailment was made even clearer for me during the winter of 2023–24, when I participated in a training programme facilitated by the Centre of Applied Jungian Studies. The programme's extensive analysis of complexes relied on the metaphor of the zombie to illustrate their nature and their disconnection from our conscious intentions and values, as well as the ways in which they can affect us.

Like the zombies we are so familiar with from movies, video games and TV series like *The Walking Dead* and *The Last of Us*, complexes act without self-reflection or appreciation of consequences. They are motivated by basic drives or instincts, operating outside the realm of morality. They are primitive, mindless, compulsive, relentless and difficult to control. Just like the undead, they tend to move in shuffling hordes, drawn together by an unconscious hunger that spreads from one to another like a psychological contagion. As Ayanna discovered, complexes infect and consume us, leading us without deviation or variation where we most fear to go.

ADDICTIONS

Like psychological complexes, addictions relate to entrenched and repetitive patterns of thought, emotion and behaviour. They operate beyond our conscious awareness and deeply impact our lives in terms of our cognitive functions, performance at work, physical health, mental well-being and how we relate to other people. Sometimes, complexes are precursors to addiction. However, addictions tend to affect us not only psychologically but also biologically and physiologically.

As physician and addiction specialist Gabor Maté's *compassionate inquiry* method reveals, addictions can be rooted in our past experiences, especially where trauma has been involved and its effects have not been properly addressed. He argues that addiction often develops to cope with the unresolved trauma, disconnecting us from uncomfortable memories and emotional pain. But such relief can only ever be short-term, making the underlying issue worse and reinforcing the addiction.

Maté emphasises the need for a contextual approach when assessing the causes of addiction. He elaborates on this in *The Myth of Normal*, co-authored with his son Daniel Maté, in which addictions and other social and health problems are viewed as symptoms of a toxic culture that undermines our basic needs for connection and meaning. Not only personal history, but social context, environment and genetics all contribute to addictive behaviours and the formation of our Shadows.

In *Dopamine Nation*, psychiatrist Anna Lembke reveals how our brain chemistry, particularly the hormone dopamine, can shape behavioural patterns that manifest as Shadows. This neurotransmitter, traditionally known as the brain's reward chemical, plays a vital role in driving not just clinical addiction but also subtly compulsive behaviours we might not initially recognise as problematic. Modern society bombards us with dopamine-triggering stimuli, from social media notifications to processed foods. These hijack our neural circuitry in ways our ancestors never experienced. This overstimulation creates a neurological imbalance that induces Shadow behaviours, including compulsive checking of our phones, mindless consumption and the constant pursuit of the next dopamine hit.

Lembke suggests that these patterns are not simply the result of trauma or weak willpower, but of our brain's adaptation to an environment of excess. When our dopamine system is unbalanced, even mentally healthy individuals can find themselves trapped in cycles of craving and dissatisfaction. Lembke highlights the importance of self-restraint, discomfort tolerance and the adoption of practices like abstinence or intentional hardship to restore balance. Understanding and working with our brain chemistry, not just our psychological wounds, is key to Shadow integration.

Self-help author Eckhart Tolle adds a spiritual perspective. He argues that addiction often arises from an unconscious refusal to face and move through our own inner pain and suffering. Tolle explains that when we are unable or unwilling to be present with and process our painful emotions, thoughts and experiences, we may turn to addictive behaviours to numb, distract or escape from that discomfort. He asserts that when we have the courage to turn toward and move through our pain, we open ourselves to healing, growth and the possibility of living with more inner peace and freedom.

This notion can become evident during times of collective trauma and isolation. During the height of the Covid pandemic, I found myself drinking alcohol more frequently than I used to. I grappled with moderation. As with most problems, my initial response was denial. Then came struggle, shame and self-loathing. I read 'quit lit' books and wanted to see if they would help me. But I failed to see myself as someone who was addicted, as I had always been able to go for weeks or even months without a drink.

Exploring my relationship with alcohol in more depth, I learned to see it as a symptom of a problem rather than the cause. In fact, it was a solution, albeit a very poor one, that I was using to help avoid feeling something I did not want to feel during a period of lockdowns, home-working and lengthy Zoom calls. It was a response to the absence of physical connection with colleagues and loved ones. With that realisation, I began a journey that involved learning to stay with my feelings rather than trying to escape them.

I also had to learn to be kinder and more compassionate toward myself. Rather than reverting to the admonishments of the inner critic, I needed to give voice to a gentler observer. "There I go again," I might tell myself when I wanted a drink. If you are struggling with any addiction or compulsion that is not serving you well, it is important to be kind to yourself and find the professional and personal support you need. In the words of musician and filmmaker Jamie Catto, "Only I alone can do this, but I can't do it alone."

Addictions are multifaceted and manifest in different ways. Substance addictions, for example, involve a dependency on drugs or alcohol. These can have a temporary soothing effect when coping with trauma or something that's missing in one's life, but soon spiral out of control, derailing careers and relationships. These addictions form when we try to regulate our internal state with external substances. Behavioural addictions like gambling and gaming, on the other hand, consume excessive time and energy, leading people to neglect social, family and work responsibilities. Even seemingly beneficial activities like exercise, work or helping others can become destructive when pursued compulsively. These *positive addictions* still reflect an underlying need to regulate emotions through external means, often at the cost of balance and well-being.

When multiple addictions intersect, they can create a particularly devastating spiral of self-destruction, as illustrated by one of Wall Street's most notorious figures. In his two-volume memoir, *The Wolf of Wall Street* and *Catching the Wolf of Wall Street*, Jordan Belfort explores how his obsession with money, success and power led him to break the law. He also reveals the effects of his addiction to quaaludes and cocaine, both of which impaired his judgement and decision-making capabilities. Belfort consequently began to take more risks, laundering money, engaging in infidelities and hiring prostitutes. His addictions overwhelmed him, with one feeding and accelerating the others until everything collapsed.

But would he have become the person he did, with his compulsive and fraudulent tendencies, had he not been socially conditioned by Wall Street's financial community? Would Elizabeth Holmes have been quite so addicted to the acquisition of wealth and the exercise of power if she had founded her company anywhere other than Silicon Valley?

In addition to impacting relationships and work performance, both substance and behavioural addictions act as financial derailers because of the costs involved in feeding such habits. Compulsive behaviours involving addictions to food, shopping or sex also can arise because of past trauma, but they tend to generate new problems, perpetuating established cycles of shame.

Process addictions like these, or workaholism or social media addiction, can inhibit personal growth and the development of healthy coping mechanisms, interfering with normal life functions. They create instability, which is also a feature of *relationship addiction*, where there is often an unhealthy pattern of dependency and self-neglect. Perhaps most destructively, addictions can lead us to objectify and dehumanise not only ourselves but others, setting the stage for even worse ethical and moral transgressions.

SEX

The intersection of power, wealth and sexual misconduct has become increasingly visible in recent years. Prominent figures across business, politics and academia have faced serious allegations and consequences, from Dominique Strauss-Kahn and Harvey Weinstein to Roger Ailes, Tariq Ramadan, Bernard Looney and Mohamed Al Fayed. Their stories often follow similar patterns, with leaders abusing their positions of authority, violating trust and derailing their careers through sexual impropriety.

Yet, the concept of sex as a derailer reveals a complex interplay of biological, psychological, social, cultural and systemic factors that extend beyond simple moral failings or lapses in judgement. In the case of people like Strauss-Kahn and Al Fayed, this phenomenon often stems from a toxic combination of entitlement, narcissism and distorted perceptions of power and consent. Here, sexual behaviour becomes a destructive force, derailing careers and relationships, damaging the reputation of the perpetrators and the organisations they are associated with.

In many cases, derailing sexual behaviour develops gradually, and may even have its roots in an individual's own past trauma. But what might begin as relatively minor transgressions can quickly evolve into more serious misconduct as people seek greater stimulation or validation, perpetuating cycles of abuse that are conducted either in person or via digital technology. This behaviour often can be accompanied by increasingly sophisticated methods of rationalisation and cognitive dissonance, allowing those who have been derailed to justify their actions despite mounting evidence of the harm they have done.

It is important to note that these sexually transgressive behaviours do not occur in a vacuum. As recent court cases and movements like *#MeToo* have highlighted, they often are enabled and sometimes even tacitly encouraged by organisational cultures, power structures and social norms that, as in Belfort's Stratton Oakmont or Harvey Weinstein's film production companies, prioritise certain forms of success over ethics. Many cases centre on the exploitation of vulnerabilities relating to gender, sexual orientation, age, race or class and are predatory in nature.

The 2022 film *Tár*, directed by Todd Field and starring Cate Blanchett, illustrates how sex can function as a derailer. The movie presents a nuanced portrait of fictional character Lydia Tár, a renowned composer and conductor, whose carefully constructed world unravels due to allegations of sexual misconduct and abuse of power. Throughout, we see how Lydia's position of authority in the upper echelons of classical music allows her to engage in manipulative and sexually exploitative behaviour, especially with young, ambitious female musicians. Yet, the film presents Lydia as a complex and flawed character rather than as a villain to be despised.

Lydia's actions reflect the entitlement often seen in powerful figures, examining how they manage to blur professional and personal boundaries to their own advantage. As the film progresses, we witness the gradual escalation of Lydia's behaviour and its consequences, learning how the accumulation of transgressions can snowball into a career-destroying scandal. Even in the face of public exposure, indisputable evidence and internal investigation, Lydia's narcissism and rationalisation prevent her from acknowledging what she has done and taking ownership of the situation.

After her fall, Lydia temporarily retreats from public view and the identity she assumed at the start of her career, taking refuge in her childhood home. This return home, where Lydia is known as Linda Tarr, is telling. It's the place where Shadows first formed, where dark impulses were initially suppressed – where, in Freudian terms, the internal conflict first emerged between the ego, the primal drive of the *id* and the social norms represented by the superego. Given the introspective and reflective nature of these scenes, we might infer that what has been repressed in youth has manifested in Lydia's problematic behaviour in adulthood, although the film remains ambivalent on this point.

Like young Linda/Lydia, by the time most of us enter the workforce for the first time, few are properly equipped for the adult world and its sexual politics. A cursory sex education class or two during our awkward teen years leaves us ignorant of what to do about the Shadow of sexuality, our sexual selves in non-intimate contexts or the subtle interplay of sexuality, attraction and consent in general human interactions. Too often, this situation trips people up, resulting in all-too-common sexual scandals. It is valuable, therefore, to consider frameworks that promote healthier approaches to sexuality and consent.

The Wheel of Consent, for example, is a tool developed by intimacy coach and chiropractor Betty Martin and explained in her book *The Art of Receiving and Giving*. It offers a framework for understanding and navigating intimate encounters. Martin's model distinguishes between four types of consensual interaction: Serve, Accept, Take and Allow. These represent two ways of giving and two ways of receiving. In *Serve*, we actively give for another's benefit, such as offering a massage. With *Accept*, we passively receive something done for our benefit, like receiving that massage. *Take* involves actively receiving for our own benefit with permission, while *Allow* means passively giving access to ourselves for another's benefit.

My understanding of the Wheel and its applications has been deepened through the work of communication coach Adam Taffler, founder of the Togetherness festival. Taffler observes how these dimensions often become confused in relationships, leading to resentment. For instance, when we give a gift expecting appreciation (Serve), but the recipient feels obligated to reciprocate (Accept), we create an unintended imbalance. By understanding these situations, we can communicate our needs and boundaries more clearly.

Taffler makes another significant observation: in professional settings, we often try to suppress or ignore sexual energy. However, this potent force remains an inherent part of human experience, inevitably influencing our interactions. Rather than denying its presence, developing awareness of how it shapes our communication, decision-making and relationships at work allows us to navigate these tensions with greater intention. This awareness can transform potential misunderstandings into opportunities for healthier professional connections.

The Wheel provides a powerful antidote to the entitled, boundary-violating behaviour that often leads to sex becoming a derailer. It emphasises that consent is not simply about saying yes or no, but about actively engaging with our own desires while respecting those of others. This is in stark contrast to the exploitative dynamics portrayed in *Tár* and observed in real-world scandals.

ANGER

Hollywood producer Harvey Weinstein's case illustrates how sexual misconduct often coexists with other destructive patterns, illustrating how different derailers interact and amplify one another. Beyond widely publicised allegations of sexual abuse, Weinstein also was notorious in the film industry for his explosive temper and aggression. This combination of predatory sexual activity and uncontrolled anger affected not only interpersonal relationships but created a toxic work culture in the organisations he led.

Weinstein's status as the head of a top production company, shepherding big-ticket movies onto the screen, contributed to a distorted sense of entitlement. His abuse of power, disregard for other people's boundaries and well-being, and lack of emotional control were all about getting what he wanted, when he wanted it. The power and authority he enjoyed as a leading figure in Hollywood fuelled both his sexual entitlement and his rage-filled outbursts, many of which derailed other people's careers before they eventually derailed his own.

The stories that have emerged about Weinstein since his downfall and imprisonment reveal examples of explosive anger in its most destructive form. But rage is just one of the many ways that anger materialises in the workplace. From the executive who intimidates subordinates with loud outbursts to the colleague who engages in passive–aggressive behaviour, anger can disrupt teams, derail projects and destroy careers. An understanding of its roots, various forms of expression and consequences is essential for developing strategies to effectively manage this potent derailer.

Connor Beaton is a coach and the founder of ManTalks. His work presents a more nuanced appreciation of anger as a derailer. Throughout his Shadow Course training programme

Beaton identifies four distinct types of anger: explosive (outwardly directed and aggressive), implosive (internally directed and self-critical), fused (where anger becomes a core part of identity) and foreign (where anger is rejected or unrecognised).

This framework helps us understand that anger as a derailer can manifest in various ways beyond the stereotypical outbursts we often associate with so-called 'angry people.' For instance, a leader with implosive anger might sabotage their own success through harsh self-criticism, while someone with foreign anger might struggle to set necessary boundaries, leading to resentment and burnout. The complex interplay of these anger patterns and their roots in personal history emerged clearly in my work with a highly successful managing director.

Despite his impressive track record, this executive's explosive anger was contributing to employee dissatisfaction and high turnover, threatening to derail his career. Standard anger management techniques had failed to address the underlying issues, and I was asked to intervene. When I had him draw a timeline of his life, reflecting on some of the highs and lows, a pattern quickly emerged. Both in his childhood home and his early work experiences, he had been exposed to very toxic environments where shouting, bullying and blame were normalised. He had absorbed this anger, and it now infected not only his work but his home life, impacting his relationship with his wife. Eventually, he agreed to leave the company and tackle the issue at a deeper level, working with a therapist to understand how family patterns were impacting him.

This case illustrates why surface-level anger management techniques often fail without deeper Shadow Work. Beaton's distinction between *shadowed anger* and *clean anger* offers valuable insights into how anger can either derail or drive positive change. Shadowed anger, like that initially displayed by the managing director, is unconscious, reactive and often dehumanising. By contrast, clean anger is focused on creating order and structure, while maintaining concern for the well-being of others. Beaton believes that the problem lies not with anger itself, but in how it is experienced and expressed.

Buddhist monk Thich Nhat Hanh suggests that anger is like mud. When well channelled, as in the notion of sacred rage, it can have utility, enabling the lotus flowers to grow, for example. Beaton explores a related idea through his concept of clean anger, which is a generative, life-giving energy akin to solar power. Clean anger, felt deeply in the heart and gut, maintains connection and compassion even while establishing firm boundaries. By staying present with our physical sensations and identifying the pain beneath our anger, we can develop a more conscious relationship with it, using it to create positive change while protecting relationships rather than destroying them. Unlike reactive anger that walls us off from others, clean anger moves us toward greater empathy and meaningful connection, allowing us to have difficult conversations while staying grounded in our bodies and committed to mutual well-being.

The skill of transforming reactive anger into this clean, generative force is essential in the workplace. As with all derailers, without self-awareness, emotional intelligence and conscious intervention, our anger can result in impaired decision-making, damaged relationships and stalled careers. Our ability to navigate and channel anger effectively becomes a key differentiator between those who succeed and those who are left behind. The latter continue to be led, albeit unconsciously in many cases, by their dark-side tendencies.

Anger, like all emotions, is somatic. It's expressed through our physiology, nervous system and gestures. How the Shadow is embodied is the topic we will turn to next.

SHADOW REFLECTIONS

- When you think about power, what images or sensations arise? How do you experience power or disempowerment in your body? What is your core understanding of power's nature? Is it coercive, benevolent or a complex interplay of the two?

- What are your deeply held beliefs about money? Can you trace these to childhood experiences? What truly drives your career choices – material success, personal fulfilment, or something more nuanced?

- How attached are you to success and external validation? Which of your strengths might you overplay? What fears prevent you from challenging the status quo or taking meaningful risks?

- In what areas of your life do you feel a lack of control? Can you identify the underlying emotions and bodily sensations that trigger compulsive behaviours? What might these be trying to communicate or protect?

- When you notice a compulsive impulse, what happens if you pause and observe instead of jumping into action? How might you reimagine these patterns as potential sources of insight rather than simply destructive forces?

- Reflect on workplace interactions where sexual energy was present. How did this energy influence your behaviour and decision-making? How can you acknowledge and channel such energy constructively while maintaining professional respect?

- How did your family system shape your relationship with anger? Is your anger a protective response, a signal of unmet needs, or perhaps a defence against the crossing of boundaries?

- Can you identify your predominant anger style? Where do you experience anger in your body? What physiological changes occur when you're angry?

- How might your perceived derailers contain hidden gifts? What would it look like to transform these challenging aspects into sources of growth and self-understanding?

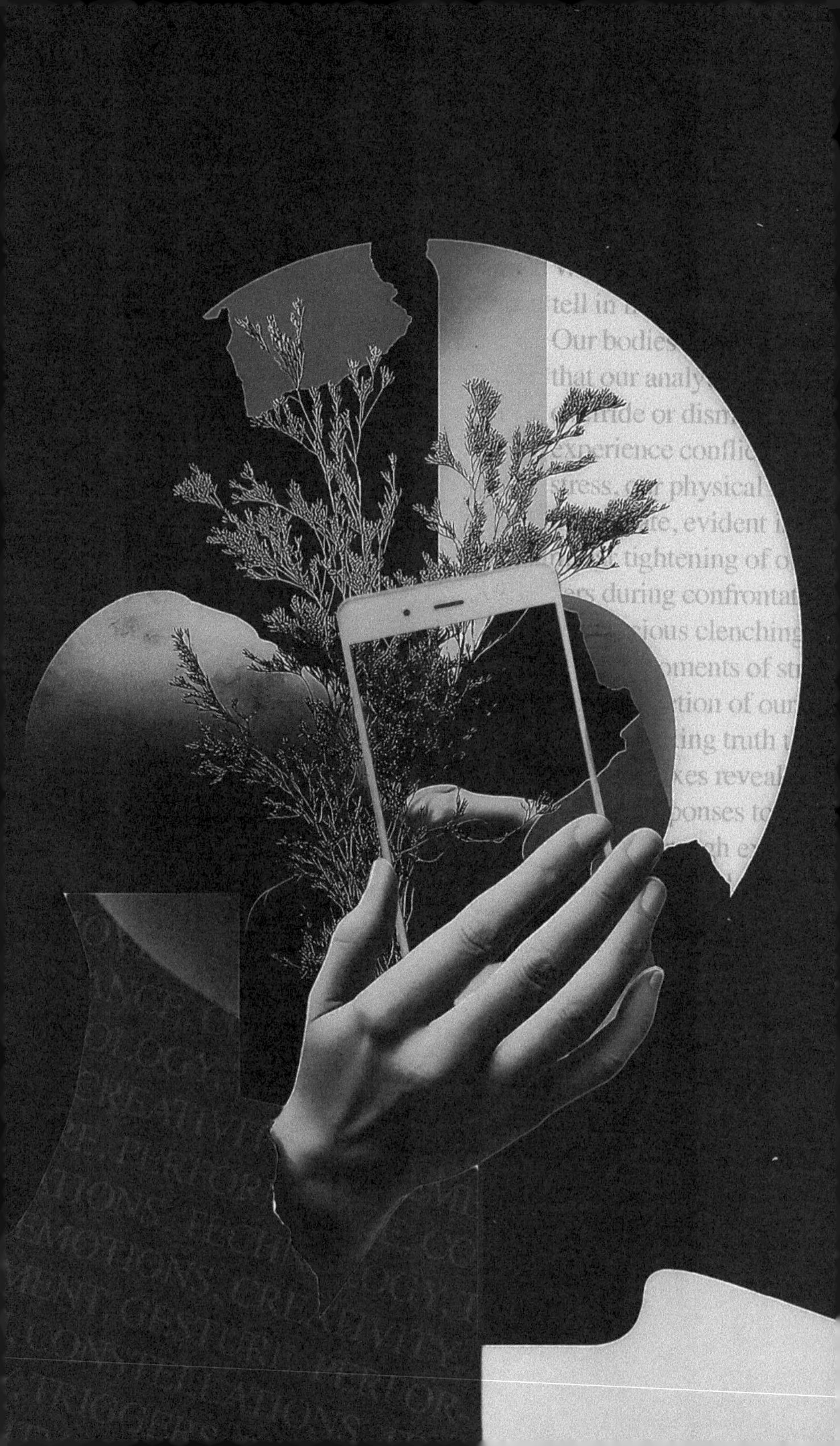

CHAPTER 5

EMBODIMENT

We aren't as solid as we once thought. We're embodied but we're also networks, expanding out into empty space, living on inside machines and in other people's heads, memories and data streams as well as flesh.

Olivia Laing
Funny Weather

My body is disconnecting from itself, losing shape and form, tangling with memory.

Daisy Johnson
Sisters

What stories does your body tell in moments of challenge?

Our bodies hold intelligence that our analytical minds often override or dismiss. When we experience conflict, trauma or stress, our physical response is immediate, evident in the familiar tightening of our shoulders during confrontation, the unconscious clenching of our jaws in moments of stress or the constriction of our throats when speaking truth to power. These reflexes reveal our learned responses to threat, developed through experiences that have shaped us. What memories and meanings might lie beneath your own physical reactions?

Since infancy, I have lived with eczema and asthma. As a baby, my body was often bandaged to protect my skin. While the essayist Susan Sontag warns us in *Illness as Metaphor* not to reduce all ailments to psychological causes, science shows clear links between our bodies and nervous systems. Through psychotherapy, I discovered that my eczema may have held a painful truth: I yearned for a soothing touch while simultaneously recoiling from contact and connection.

What physical patterns might be speaking to you with similar persistence and wisdom? While this isn't true for every illness, disregarding the body's intelligence would be unwise. My own symptoms related to a pre-verbal infancy experience of abandonment, and as I grew older, my body carried reliable signals of my emotional state. Even today, my eczema flares and my asthma attacks are more frequent during periods of stress.

Research by trauma experts reveals how profoundly our earliest experiences shape both our psyche and our physiology. In *The Body Keeps the Score*, psychiatrist Bessel van der Kolk tells us trauma lodges in the body, creating lasting physiological changes that manifest in our automatic responses. Similarly, Gabor Maté's *When the Body Says No* shows how stress and unexpressed emotions can influence our physical health.

That reflexive shoulder hunch when criticised, habitual smile when feeling threatened, unconscious crossing of arms during challenging discussions – these are physical manifestations of our life stories. How might understanding these embodied patterns offer new pathways for Shadow integration and leadership development?

We carry our Shadows in our bodies whether we realise it or not. It is evident in our tension, our illnesses and our stress responses. But there is a significant difference between this unconscious embodiment and the practice of consciously inhabiting our full selves, including those aspects we typically push away. This awareness opens new possibilities for transformation.

Shadow Work helps us recognise powerful patterns in organisational life. A leader's physical habits, such as constant pacing during meetings, might be interpreted as enthusiastic energy when they really signal discomfort with vulnerability and stillness. Their frenetic movement can create an atmosphere of anxiety that ripples through the entire organisation. What might our own physical presence be communicating to others? How might our responses to social pressures become embedded and passed down through institutions and cultures?

The 2024 film *The Substance* explores this idea through its reimagining of Hans Christian Andersen's story *The Shadow*. Elisabeth Sparkle (Demi Moore) is a Hollywood star and aerobics instructor who is fired from her TV show on the day of her 50th birthday. When Elisabeth uses a black-market serum known as The Substance, she spawns a flawless, younger doppelgänger, Sue (Margaret Qualley). The two must switch consciousness every seven days to avoid unintended side effects.

Sue becomes an overnight sensation and is offered Elisabeth's role on her old TV show, as well as a prestigious New Year's Eve show. She lives an increasingly hedonistic life of casual sex and parties. Meanwhile, Elisabeth becomes more reclusive and self-loathing, doubting her own beauty and worth. Eventually, Sue turns against Elisabeth, seeking to destroy her. Instead, they achieve mutual destruction, creating the mutated body of 'Monstro Elisasue.'

This darkly satirical body horror film explores how Elisabeth's struggle with being considered too old for her profession resonates with contemporary anxieties about ageing and value, particularly in industries that fetishise youth. As the perfect Shadow embodies society's impossible standards of eternal youth and beauty, the film reveals how internalised expectations take physical form, transforming psychological violence into bodily menace.

Societal pressures shape not just individuals but entire organisational cultures, particularly in environments that demand the suppression of certain emotions or experiences. The effects of systemic oppression, cultural trauma and institutional power become visible in the ways we collectively carry and conduct ourselves. These forces affect not just individual bodies, but our shared patterns of movement and response.

Their impact becomes clear in leadership presence. Some leaders seem to naturally command attention, while others struggle to be seen even when speaking from a position of authority. In the context of modern leadership, where we are often encouraged to 'live from the neck up,' paying attention to our bodily wisdom offers new pathways for development. That tension in your shoulders could be protecting an old wound. That recurring headache during conflict might be your body's way of signalling unacknowledged anger. Those chronic digestive issues flaring up during periods of change could be expressing fears that have escaped your conscious awareness.

As we explore the relationship between embodiment and Shadow Work, we need to stop treating our bodies as mere vehicles for our minds. Instead, we need to understand them as intelligent systems that hold and express our full story, including those aspects we have pushed into the Shadows. This chapter explores how we can develop a more nuanced and respectful relationship with our physical selves, recognising that our bodies are not problems to be solved but allies in our journey toward wholeness.

TRIGGERS

In the case of trauma, it stems from an experience that overwhelms an individual's or a society's capacity to cope, making a lasting psychological and somatic impression. Emotional and physical reactions can be triggered long after the fact by stimuli that serve as gateways to unresolved past experiences.

For example, Tunde, a regional pharmaceutical director, found himself unable to breathe properly during quarterly review meetings. He noticed that his chest felt constricted and his posture contracted, making him feel weak and unable to contribute effectively. Through therapy, he discovered that these physiological responses stemmed from childhood experiences of being harshly judged by authority figures. His body's reaction – shallow breathing, tensed muscles, racing heart – triggered self-doubt that impacted his executive presence.

Such a pattern is consistent with my colleague Francis Briers's theory about embodied leadership. Briers highlights how understanding and working with embodied patterns can interrupt cycles of stress and reactivity, helping leaders manage trauma responses and operate more effectively in high-pressure environments. Embodiment, according to Briers, also allows leaders to connect to their values and purpose, with development of their somatic capacities complementing their cognitive awareness.

Working with embodied triggers and Shadows requires conscious awareness and acknowledgement of physical and emotional responses. This might involve practices like mindfulness body scanning, where individuals sequentially focus on physical sensations in different parts of the body. Based on a traditional Buddhist meditation technique, this can help reduce stress, manage pain, regulate emotions and strengthen the connection between body and mind. Or, there are movement therapies that allow for the expression and release of trapped emotions and energies.

A particularly effective centring practice for leaders is the ABC (Awareness, Breathing/Balance, Core) method. It begins with cultivating awareness of sensations and surroundings, then focuses on breathing patterns and physical balance, concluding with attention to the body's central axis and core areas. This mindfulness exercise, which also draws on ancient Buddhist contemplative practices, can be especially valuable when feeling triggered or off-centre, as Shadow behaviours often emerge during times of stress and disconnection from our centred state.

Learning about physical and mental exhaustion and how they can trigger embodied Shadows is essential. Through somatic methods that promote body awareness and self-regulation, we can develop resilience to counteract their effects. When we are depleted, our usual defences and coping mechanisms are weakened, making us more susceptible to the emergence of repressed emotions and unresolved traumas. In the Alcoholics Anonymous movement, they use the acronym HALT (Hungry, Angry, Lonely, Tired) to indicate how unwanted behaviour may be influenced by our current state. Any feeling of vulnerability can cause heightened emotions, resurfacing old fears and anxieties. It also can induce physical symptoms that echo past traumas. Someone who has experienced burnout, for example, might find that extreme tiredness triggers feelings of inadequacy or failure, even in unrelated situations.

Recognising exhaustion as a trigger is crucial for Shadow Work, as it highlights the importance of energy management and self-care in maintaining psychological balance. The Uber board's 2017 decision to recommend a leave of absence for CEO Travis Kalanick highlighted organisational recognition of how sustained pressure affects leadership capacity. Prior to the board's decision, Kalanick had exhibited increasingly erratic behaviour. There were reports of him encouraging a hostile work culture, spying on competitors and responding aggressively to media criticism. A boating incident that caused his mother's death and serious injury to his father added to the stress he was experiencing.

At companies across all sectors, we see how unrelenting stress without adequate recovery creates conditions where suppressed emotions and behaviours are more likely to surface. This has led to increased awareness of why organisations need strategies for managing energy levels and creating buffers against the involuntary emergence of Shadow elements during times of intense pressure. While they can provide structural support, individuals also need practical tools for managing these triggers.

Breath work practices offer one such method for engaging with embodied Shadows. By consciously altering our breathing patterns, we may access repressed emotions and memories, potentially bringing aspects of the Shadow into conscious awareness. This physiological approach to Shadow work highlights the intimate connection between our mental states and our physical processes, providing a practical tool for self-exploration and integration.

It is important to note, however, that the process of integrating embodied Shadows is not about eliminating triggers or becoming immune to trauma. Rather, it is about developing a more conscious relationship with these aspects of our experience. To achieve integration involves acknowledging and accepting the ways in which past experiences have shaped us in an embodied way, while recognising our capacity for growth and transformation. As leaders, adopting a 'trauma-informed' approach means understanding how stress and adversity impact behaviour and decision-making. We need to be able to create psychologically safe environments for our colleagues and recognise when they require additional support.

EMOTION

The journey toward both personal integration and leadership effectiveness requires us to develop literacy about our own emotions and those of other people, understanding how they are connected to the body. Any emotion, from happiness to grief, from elation to disappointment, can be deemed contextually appropriate. But despite our attempts to suppress them, they can manifest in non-verbal ways without our conscious awareness.

Most of us have a very limited lexicon when it comes to our emotions. According to the Sentiment and Emotion Lexicons published by the National Research Council Canada (NRC), we rely on eight basic emotion labels (anger, fear, anticipation, trust, surprise, sadness, joy and disgust) and two concerning sentiments (negative and positive). But this ignores the multifaceted nature of experience, which cannot be easily encapsulated in single words.

In fact, our emotions often are embodied as metaphors. We speak about 'butterflies in the stomach,' 'a punch in the gut,' or something as painful as 'a kick in the nuts.' In *The Dictionary of Obscure Sorrows*, multidisciplinarian John Koenig seeks to expand this emotional vocabulary, while in *Atlas of the Heart*, social work expert and management scholar Brené Brown explores language and emotions that reflect human connection.

Our bodies show our emotions through posture, behavioural tics, facial expressions, gestures and physiological responses like sweating, increased heart rate, shortness of breath and nausea. Our unexpressed anger may be visible in our clenched jaw, rigid shoulders, fisted hands, sadness in our downcast eyes, shame in the way we cower. Our bodies are just as eloquent as our words. Popular culture plays on this constantly. For example, Bruce Banner's body transforms into the Hulk when he is angry, while Carrie's telekinetic powers are activated by her experience of intense emotions like anger or fear.

In works like *Feeling and Knowing*, neuroscientist Antonio Damasio has added to our understanding of emotions and their embodiment. For Damasio, consciousness arises from the interaction between the brain, body and environment, with emotions and feelings playing a key role in this process. Our emotions are unconscious neural responses to stimuli, while feelings arise when we become aware of these bodily changes.

Damasio's work challenges the traditional view that emotions interfere with reason. With his somatic marker hypothesis, he suggests that past emotional experiences create bodily sensations associated with specific situations. These influence future choices and behaviours. Emotions not only result in faster decision-making, but help us navigate complex and uncertain situations and steer us toward those choices least likely to disadvantage us.

The somatic marker hypothesis is relevant to leadership in several ways. It highlights the importance of emotional intelligence for leaders. By developing greater self-awareness, leaders can appreciate how their emotional states influence both themselves and others. Such awareness helps them enhance their social skills and connect more effectively with colleagues. By acknowledging what their bodies are telling them, and integrating this with cognitive information, leaders can make more balanced decisions and improve their resilience and stress management as they become adept at understanding the physiological basis of their emotions.

Emotionally intelligent leaders also are more attuned to non-verbal cues and can gain valuable insights about their employees' emotional state. By observing body language and other physical indicators – including what psychologist Paul Ekman refers to as *microexpressions* of shock, fear, anger, disgust, sadness and happiness – leaders can identify underlying issues or conflicts that may not be openly discussed. However, we should not forget that it is easy to misread body language and facial expressions, misinterpreting the emotional state of others or even projecting our own onto them. This challenge requires leaders to develop their observational skills through practice and careful attention to patterns and context.

This skill becomes even more critical in today's hybrid working environment, where leaders must accurately read non-verbal cues both in person and online. Detecting even the smallest shifts in facial expressions over time and in different contexts can help us sense and respond to changing emotional patterns.

Understanding the impact of emotional contagion is also useful. Emotions can spread rapidly from one person to another through unconscious mimicry of facial expressions, body language and vocal patterns. Leaders who are aware of this process can consciously model positive emotional states and foster a supportive work environment. A simple smile, nod or upbeat intonation all can have a positive ripple effect.

Emotional awareness can help leaders address problems proactively. Through co-regulation, where people naturally influence and stabilise each other's emotional states through social interaction, leaders can nurture an environment that supports individual and collective well-being. This might involve implementing regular check-ins, encouraging open dialogue about feelings or introducing practices that help employees become more aware of their bodily sensations and emotions. For example, some Japanese companies have incorporated *shinrin-yoku* ('forest bathing') into their employee wellness programmes. This involves mindful time in nature, recognising the need for emotional regulation and stress reduction through physical experiences.

The embodiment of Shadows and their associated emotions also can surface in organisational cultures. Just as individuals repress certain facets of themselves, organisations can develop Shadow aspects, whereby certain emotions or behaviours are perceived to be unacceptable. This can lead to a disconnection between the official organisational culture and the lived experience of employees.

Leaders who are willing to acknowledge and work with these Shadow aspects can create more authentic and resilient organisations. At Microsoft, for example, when Satya Nadella took over from Steve Ballmer as CEO, he opted to tackle head-on the company's Shadow culture of internal competition and defensiveness. By openly acknowledging these issues and promoting both empathy and Carol Dweck's concept of a growth mindset, Nadella helped transform Microsoft's internal culture, leading to improved employee satisfaction and business performance. This initiative transformed Microsoft from a 'know it all' culture to a 'learn it all' one, where curiosity, humility and a willingness to learn are highly valued qualities.

This kind of cultural transformation requires a delicate balance. While openness to emotions is vital, leaders must also maintain appropriate boundaries and professional conduct. Psychological techniques like emotional labelling, where the emotions we experience are simply identified and named, can be useful. This can help maintain the necessary distance while enhancing self-awareness and emotional regulation, as well as problem-solving, decision-making and communication capabilities. Recognising our emotions and understanding where they come from can make better leaders of us all.

CREATIVITY

It is all too easy to forget that there are gifts to be found in the Shadows. Jung's notion of the Golden Shadow represents those positive qualities that, as individuals and communities, we either have failed to recognise in ourselves or disowned. These might include untapped creativity, natural leadership abilities or deep emotional wisdom that we have somehow come to suppress or ignore. Often, we project these golden qualities onto others, admiring in them the very talents and capabilities that lie dormant within ourselves. This projection can manifest as deep admiration for others' achievements while doubting our own potential, or as an inexplicable attraction to certain roles or activities that we believe are not for us.

But by embracing and embodying what previously was hidden, it is possible to harness our potential for innovation, artistic expression and creativity, as well as effective leadership. The journey of discovering our Golden Shadow often reveals that our greatest perceived limitations are, in fact, gateways to our most powerful capabilities.

Oprah Winfrey, the groundbreaking media executive, television host, producer, actress and philanthropist, has often been hailed for her inspiration and empowerment of others. However, her journey to fame and fortune involved numerous challenges. Like many successful individuals, Winfrey grappled with aspects of herself that she initially suppressed in pursuit of success.

Growing up in poverty and enduring a traumatic childhood, which included episodes of sexual abuse, Winfrey learned early on to suppress her true emotions and feelings. She became adept at presenting a polished, confident persona to the world, hiding the pain and vulnerability that lay beneath the surface. Yet, it was precisely these suppressed aspects of herself that would ultimately fuel her creativity and drive, including her celebrated performance as Sofia in the film version of *The Color Purple*.

Winfrey's ability to empathise deeply with others, speak openly about her own struggles and champion the stories of marginalised people became the foundation of her success. As she embraced these once hidden parts of herself, Winfrey found the courage to share her own story with humility and vulnerability – pioneering the 'confessional talk show' form – and inspiring millions around the world to do the same. She showed people how they could make sense of their own trauma and work with it. In so doing, they too could develop the capacity to heal their wounds and transform them into gifts. Her story exemplifies what Jung called the 'Wounded Healer' archetype. This powerful concept, inspired by the centaur Chiron of ancient Greek mythology, recognises that true healing capacity often emerges from our own wounds. Chiron became a legendary teacher and healer precisely because he was poisoned by Hercules's arrow.

In the case of musician David Bowie, his assumption of numerous personas throughout his career – including Ziggy Stardust, Aladdin Sane and the Thin White Duke – illustrates the creative power of embodying multiple aspects of the Golden Shadow. Bowie constantly reinvented himself. On each occasion, this allowed him to explore different facets of his artistry. Through changes in musical genre, costume, hair, makeup and sexual identity, Bowie embraced fluidity and impermanence, pushing into territory where many artists dared not venture for fear of losing their status and established audience. But Bowie repeatedly shed old personas and styles to emerge phoenix-like with innovative new looks, recordings and stage shows that attracted even wider audiences. This resulted in a diverse and influential body of work, affecting not only music but fashion and design, inspiring many others in these creative fields.

Fluidity is also central to architect Zaha Hadid's engagement with the Golden Shadow. Her structures embody a different vision of space and form than the rectilinear designs produced by many of the men who have long dominated her field. By bringing disowned aspects of architectural creativity to the forefront, Hadid managed to achieve personal success while also expanding the possibilities of what architecture can accomplish.

Buildings like the Vitra Fire Station, Bridge Pavilion, London Aquatics Centre, Al-Janoub Stadium and 520 West 28th reflect her refusal to be constrained by conventional ideas about architecture. Her work challenges the very notion of built space, embodying a fluidity and dynamism that many in the field had rejected as impractical or impossible. Like Winfrey and Bowie, Hadid showed that when we fully embody our creative potential, regardless of societal expectations and norms, we can transform the world and open new possibilities for others to enjoy.

This embodiment of the Golden Shadow often manifests through groundbreaking creative expression, as evidenced by the accomplishments of these celebrated individuals. However, the process of surfacing and leveraging hidden potential is not limited to a select few. As illustrated by art educator Betty Edwards in her book *Drawing on the Right Side of the Brain*, it is a capacity we all possess. With an argument that echoes psychiatrist Iain McGilchrist's findings in *The Master and His Emissary*, Edwards suggests that we all have the innate ability to draw, but this skill often lies dormant due to our education system's emphasis on left-brain, analytical thinking.

As touched on in Chapter 1, McGilchrist maintains that the left hemisphere's dominance in modern society has led to a fragmented, decontextualised view of the world, while the right hemisphere offers a more holistic, embodied understanding.

For Edwards, creative potential is often suppressed because right-hemisphere preferences for spatial, holistic and intuitive thinking are overshadowed by the left-hemisphere approach to problem-solving and self-expression. The reintegration of right-hemisphere modes of perception and processing, of methods we have learned to disown and suppress, offers an opportunity for a more balanced and creative approach to life and work.

This holistic approach to creativity extends beyond cognitive processes to encompass the full spectrum of human experience, including our wounds and traumas. The dancer Gabrielle Roth recognised this transformative potential when working with students. Whenever she was confronted with stories of past trauma, Roth would respond with both compassion and empowering humour, declaring, "Wonderful, I expect great art from you!" Far from trivialising trauma, she understood that creative expression could serve as a powerful vehicle for healing, not just for the individual, but for the broader community. In Roth's vision, art transcends mere artefacts to become an approach to life itself, a way of transforming our wounds into wisdom.

Shadow Work teaches us that complete healing may remain eternally beyond our reach. We are, after all, always becoming, never finished. Yet, through conscious engagement with our Shadows, we can learn to teach and create from our scars rather than unconsciously acting from our wounds.

MOVEMENT, GESTURE, PERFORMANCE

Our Shadows live in our bodies, emerging through our physical presence and the ways we move and behave. I learned this lesson early, working with deaf young people when I was eighteen. That experience showed me how limited spoken words could be, and how much meaning we convey through our bodies and gestures. A simple word like 'happy' wasn't just signed, it was embodied with a genuine smile. Even people's names were communicated through gestures, which could be either delightful or dismaying depending on the association.

The bodily awareness of our Shadows appears in countless ways. Think about how your posture changes when you are feeling confident or insecure, or how your breathing shifts when you are either angry or at peace. Our bodies tell stories that our words might hide. Learning to read and work with these physical signals opens new paths to self-discovery and growth.

The theatre provides powerful tools for exploring these bodily dimensions of our Shadows, as I discovered in my conversations with Richard Olivier about his Olivier Mythodrama programme. He shared a pivotal experience from 1997 at the reconstructed Globe Theatre, where he directed a production of Shakespeare's *Henry V*, starring Mark Rylance. "I learned a huge amount from the practice," he told me, describing how they took the all-male cast to an abandoned air base for three intense days. "We all stayed in character and embodied the scenes and the intention of the scenes. It was the touchpoint for me that the wisdom of myth could be embodied." The production's success proved the power of this approach.

Olivier and his colleagues subsequently refined and developed what had been learned from the experience. In 2003, he led 50 CEOs at the World Economic Forum through a three-hour

'Archetypes at Work' session, using *Henry V* as a lens for examining leadership challenges. The timing was significant. In the wake of the Enron financial fraud scandal, many executives were addressing their own 'dark night of the soul', struggling to reconcile the public and private faces of leadership. Through Shakespeare's characters and themes, they found a safe space to explore questions of purpose, vision and authentic leadership.

Today, Olivier continues this work, using Shakespearean plays and archetypes to examine different facets of leadership embodiment and effectiveness, and their impact on organisational life. This connects deeply with my own experience in Ontological Coaching through the Newfield Network coaching group, where I learned how different leadership archetypes could be explored through the body.

For instance, if you want to access your inner sovereign, that source of calm authority, then stand tall, push your shoulders back and imagine wearing a crown and heavy cloak. You will notice immediate changes in your posture, breathing and emotional state. But if you need to access the warrior archetype, you should adopt the focused, determined posture of someone navigating a crowded street with purpose, like an arrow aimed at its target. The lover archetype, by contrast, requires an open, welcoming posture – heart exposed, hands relaxed at your sides – while the playful fool type depends on loose, fluid movements and a light touch embodying flexibility. Using our bodies to change our states and dispositions can be a powerful way to increase our leadership repertoire.

Voice coach Patsy Rodenburg's Three Circles of Energy framework offers another perspective on physical presence. During my training with her, I learned how powerful presence exists in the body before a word is spoken. She cited as an example the stage and screen actor Judi Dench. Though small in stature, Dench commands attention the moment she enters a room, a technique she used to powerful effect in her role as intelligence service chief M in a series of James Bond films. This understanding of embodied presence guides my own coaching practice. When executives are stuck in rigid thinking patterns, I sometimes ask them to shift their physical state, putting their hands behind their heads and feet up on their desks. The laughter this posture generates often achieves what hours of serious discussion cannot, freeing them to think and feel differently.

The practice of Social Presencing Theatre, developed by Arawana Hayashi at the Presencing Institute, takes this embodied exploration to a deeper level. Through techniques like 4D Mapping, participants create physical representations of their inner landscape and systemic relationships in the room, and then explore what they can learn that will help them better understand challenges and find solutions. This approach reveals connections and patterns that might remain hidden in conventional discussion. It is particularly powerful for exploring collective Shadows that emerge in group and organisational contexts.

Japanese butoh dancers offer yet another perspective, deliberately embracing what society often deems dark or grotesque. Their work reminds us that our Shadows are not static. They shift and flow like our physical and emotional states. Through raw, authentic movement, they push audiences to confront what is hidden and repressed in both individual and collective experience.

What connects all these approaches is the recognition that our Shadows are not just mental constructs, but are deeply woven into our physical experience. By working with our bodies through movement, gesture and performance, we can access and integrate aspects of ourselves that might otherwise remain hidden. This bodily awakening naturally extends beyond us, reshaping how we move through the world and relate to others.

When we learn to move with and through our Shadows, we expand our capacity for authentic self-expression. We discover that our bodies carry wisdom that our minds alone might miss, opening new possibilities for growth and connection. This embodied approach to Shadow Work enables a more integrated and authentic expression of self, not only as individuals but as communities working toward collective transformation.

CONSTELLATIONS

Systemic Constellations therapy, an approach pioneered by the Catholic missionary and psychoanalyst Bert Hellinger and further developed by practitioners like Judith Hemming, reveals how our individual Shadows connect to larger patterns. Systems like families, organisations and cultures have their own dynamics, memories and unresolved issues that can surface in our lives. This is particularly evident in cases of inherited trauma, as seen in descendants of slaves, Holocaust survivors and Indigenous peoples subjected to colonialism, reminding us that not all the Shadows we confront are entirely personal.

The constellations practice involves creating physical representations of systemic elements in clearly defined settings. When working in groups, these 'representatives' are usually other people, but they can be physical objects when we work alone. Each element is placed intuitively in relation to the others, creating a living map of how the system works. What makes this practice particularly relevant to embodied Shadow Work is its emphasis on physical sensation, movement and non-verbal communication.

The power of this approach becomes clear through practical application. I once coached a doctor facing a difficult choice between two options. We wrote each option on pieces of paper and placed them in different parts of the room. When he stood on each option, observing his body's reactions, the contrast was striking. Though his mind remained uncertain, one option made him feel lighter, more open and stable, while the other created noticeable discomfort. This physical exploration provided valuable additional insight to inform his decision.

Embodied knowledge extends beyond individual experience. In constellation work, people in representative roles often report physical sensations, emotions and impulses that seem to come from beyond themselves. They relate less to their personal experience than to whatever it is they are representing. Hellinger called this phenomenon the *knowing field*, suggesting a form of knowledge that transcends individual consciousness. When applied to Shadow Work, it can reveal how certain Shadow aspects are connected to systemic loyalties and to what remains hidden and unspoken.

The world of team sports offers a vivid illustration of how constellations operate in practice. In football, for example, the team's formation on the pitch creates a living constellation, with each player's position relative to the others influencing the flow of the game. When a manager shifts from a 4-4-2 formation of offense and defence players to a 3-5-2 one, they are essentially rearranging this constellation to alter team dynamics and performance.

These systemic relationships in football extend beyond tactical formations. Professional teams often develop family-like relationships, with senior players adopting parental roles and younger ones embodying those of children and siblings, all of which can affect team performance. At the international level, teams carry the weight of historical and cultural expectations, too. The Brazilian national team's style of play, for example, is influenced by the cultural mandate of *jogo bonito* ('the beautiful game'), emphasising individual players' style and creativity. These influences extend beyond the current squad to encompass national football heritage and the expectations of millions.

The physical expression of such systemic patterns emerges through constellation mapping, whether we're working with sports teams, business organisations or personal decisions. As we manoeuvre representatives, we gain insights by observing subtle cues in the systemic picture, noting patterns, clustering, dispersion, proximity and gaps. The movements that emerge spontaneously in a constellation – such as a representative turning away, reaching out or sinking to the ground – reveal core truths about the relationships and underlying forces at play. These physical expressions often bypass our usual mental defences, allowing hidden or repressed aspects to emerge into consciousness.

In her organisational work, Hemming emphasises the importance of 'acknowledging what is,' a principle that aligns closely with the acceptance and integration central to Shadow Work. By physically embodying different elements of a system or aspects of ourselves, we can uncover hidden relationships and begin to shift entrenched patterns.

Constellations add an important systemic dimension to our understanding of embodied Shadows. They invite us to consider how our personal Shadows might be entwined with larger patterns, highlighting how movement and gesture can reveal these connections. This systemic perspective reminds us that embodied Shadow Work ripples outward, influencing the larger systems of which we are a part. The body becomes a bridge between the individual and the collective unconscious, while our embodied explorations extend into a wider web of relationships. They reach beyond human systems to affect our environment and the technologies we use as well.

TECHNOLOGY

Technology acts as a powerful mirror, showing us both our collective Shadow aspects and our Golden Shadow potentials. We see this most clearly in our digital personas and online behaviour. Social media platforms become stages where we simultaneously project idealised versions of ourselves while expressing Shadow elements through snark, trolling, harassment or compulsive validation-seeking.

Yet, these same platforms reveal Golden Shadow aspects through authentic self-expression and community-building that might feel unsafe in physical spaces. For example, a teenager struggling with gender identity might find acceptance and understanding in online communities before feeling safe expressing themselves in the physical world.

Artificial Intelligence (AI) systems, particularly large language models (LLMs), encode both the capabilities and limitations we programme into them. They exhibit remarkable abilities in areas like pattern recognition, creativity and problem-solving, while also absorbing and reproducing our societal biases and prejudices. These systems reveal something profound about our collective potential and our blind spots.

Tomas Chamorro-Premuzic warns in *I, Human*, that this efficiency comes at a cost. He notes that AI may be simplifying our lives in ways that reduce human creativity and adaptability, making us more predictable and less distinctively human. The challenge lies in reclaiming and developing human qualities such as curiosity, empathy and emotional intelligence rather than allowing technology to flatten these qualities.

The phenomenon of digital disembodiment represents another notable Shadow aspect of our technological age. As sociologist Sherry Turkle argues in *Alone Together*, even our most sophisticated virtual spaces cannot replicate the neurological and emotional benefits of genuine human presence. Our devices and interfaces strip away fundamental elements of the human experience, including touch, subtle facial expressions and the unconscious synchronisation of breathing and movement that occurs between people sharing physical space.

Even a phone visible during a conversation can significantly decrease rapport between people, creating an invisible barrier to genuine connection. However, this very limitation has sparked a Golden Shadow response, with a growing appreciation for physical presence and authentic connection. The emergence of movements like 'raw dogging' (the practice of enduring long-haul flights without any digital distractions, movies, music, books or snacks) and the intentional creation of tech-free zones represent attempts to reclaim embodied experience.

Corporate technologies capture both Shadow and Golden aspects of our economic systems. The gig economy and surveillance capitalism reveal Shadow elements of exploitation and control, reducing human labour to data points and algorithms. Wellness technologies, criticised as 'McMindfulness,' often commercialise genuine human needs for contemplation and inner peace. Yet within these same systems lie seeds of potential transformation. They include the democratisation of economic opportunity and the possibility of transparent and equitable systems, as well as tools that could genuinely support psychological well-being when used conscientiously.

Virtual and augmented reality spaces enable unprecedented exploration of identity and consciousness. These technologies can become platforms for acting out Shadow impulses without apparent consequences. They also provide safe spaces for psychological integration and creative expression. An individual might explore aspects of their personality in virtual worlds that they have been afraid to acknowledge in physical reality, leading to greater self-acceptance and integration. These immersive technologies highlight our capacity for both destructive and transformative possibilities.

The challenge we face is not in rejecting technology's Shadow aspects. Rather, it lies in consciously integrating both its light and dark potential. This means developing digital tools that enhance rather than replace embodied human connection. It requires creating spaces that support authentic self-expression while acknowledging our Shadow elements. We need to develop systems that reflect our highest collective potential while remaining grounded in the full spectrum of human complexity.

Healthy technological development requires neither demonising nor idealising digital tools, but understanding them as mirrors of our complete human experience, including both our wounds and our gifts. As Turkle and Chamorro-Premuzic suggest, this requires conscious cultivation of our uniquely human qualities while thoughtfully integrating technological tools that enhance rather than diminish our humanity.

SHADOW REFLECTIONS

- What physiological signals does your body send before your mind becomes conscious of a trigger? Can you map the somatic landscape of your immediate reactions – the downturned mouth, clenched fists, averted gaze?

- How can you expand your emotional vocabulary to more precisely locate and express your bodily experiences? Experiment with describing feelings through their physical sensations, creating language that bridges inner experience and external communication.

- Try keeping a Trigger Diary for several weeks. What patterns emerge when you attentively track your bodily responses, emotions and thoughts? How might this practice increase your self-understanding?

- How do you transform internal wounds or unprocessed experiences through creative mediums? Explore a form of expression that allows your body to speak, whether through drawing, movement, craft or writing.

- How do your posture, movements and gestures reveal your inner landscape? What unconscious bodily patterns might be communicating something deeper about your attitudes and ways of being?

- If you were to represent your current inner dilemma using human representatives, what positions, relationships or dynamics might emerge? How might this external mapping reveal hidden insights?

- What internal experiences or Shadow aspects have you found ways to externalise or make tangible? What methods have you used to bring the invisible into conscious awareness?

- How does your digital presence reflect or differ from your physical self? What aspects of yourself do you curate or conceal in online interactions?

- Can you detect patterns in how your technology use influences your sense of connection to yourself and others? What might your online communication reveal about your inner state?

its presence that Pranayama embodies it...
...ound about Shadow Work itself. It is not about eliminating our...
...s or even fully resolving them, but rather in standing with...
...areness, we become more fully...
...owledged aspects...
...yeness. This discord...
...ce that composer...
...tual bypassing that...
...s. As Saint Irenaeus...
...od is a man fully alive. This refl...
...from complete acceptance, but is...
...ing everything, both light and...
...omise of Shadow Work...
...but the embrace of...
...ompassion and...
...at we are both...
...ther. The journey of Shadow Work...
...perfection, not about...
...rly those aspects that we...
...e. Ju...

CHAPTER 6

LIVING THE SHADOW LIFE

A life's work is not a series of stepping-stones, onto which we calmly place our feet, but more like an ocean crossing where there is no path, only a heading, a direction, in conversation with the elements.

David Whyte
Consolations

Life is not a problem but an opportunity. An opportunity for eternal growth, for using every moment and every experience no matter how joyful or painful to enlighten one's consciousness ever further.

Shiv Sengupta
Putting Wings on a Caterpillar

What would happen if you stopped running? If you turned around and faced what you have been avoiding. Not just the fears and doubts, but the unlived lives, the roads not taken, the versions of yourself that you have dismissed as impractical, irresponsible or impossible? As Jung reminded us, until we make the unconscious conscious, we will call it fate, and it will direct our lives. This journey of confronting our Shadows holds the key to unlocking our full potential.

Throughout this book, we have explored how our Shadows shape us. What began as an exploration of our supposed dark side has revealed something far more nuanced and profound. The Shadows, we have discovered, are simply what is hidden. They are neither inherently dark nor light, but are those aspects of ourselves we have relegated to the unconscious. These can include qualities we once thought unacceptable, as well as our greatest gifts.

This notion of embracing Shadow lives, those unlived possibilities within us, is encapsulated by the story of the young Siddhartha Gautama, who would later become the Buddha. His father, King Śuddhodana, created an entirely artificial environment for his son, surrounding him only with youth, beauty and pleasure. All signs of ageing, illness and death were hidden from the young prince on Śuddhodana's orders. But this Shadow-free artifice would have deep psychological and spiritual consequences when Siddhartha finally encountered the realities his father had hidden from him, catalysing a transformative journey from protected privilege to enlightened awareness.

One of my favourite novels is Herman Hesse's novel *Siddhartha*, which explores the power of an individual finding their own path rather than adhering to any single teaching or tradition. Hesse's Siddhartha moves from ascetic spirituality to worldly pleasure, from merchant and householder to ferryman, each identity containing its own truth but none offering the complete answer. It is only at the end – contemplating a river, which he realises is always moving and always changing, yet always there and always the same – that he looks back and sees that each part of his journey was interconnected, meaningful, essential. His story reminds us that our own paths are rarely linear or predictable. We may need to inhabit multiple lives, try on different selves, before we can integrate all aspects of our experience into a meaningful whole.

My own journey mirrors this pattern. It began with a calling to priesthood before I took on diverse roles in hospitality, NGO work, banking, entrepreneurship, education and corporate leadership. Throughout my various career transitions there has been a constant thread involving my search for fulfilment and meaningful contribution. While I may be far from enlightenment, and it is not my aspiration, this winding path has enriched my life immeasurably, fostering genuine personal growth at each turn.

The musician Nick Cave is another who has integrated seemingly contradictory lives, undergoing a transformation from chaotic hedonist to contemplative artist. During the early days with his bands The Birthday Party and The Bad Seeds, Cave embodied a wild, almost possessed persona, performing with feral intensity, diving into audiences and living in a heroin-induced haze that nearly claimed his life in the 1980s. His early lyrics were full of Gothic violence and Biblical fury.

Rather than disowning this turbulent past, Cave's later work synthesised it. The raw emotional power of his early years found new expression in works of startling tenderness and wisdom. His love songs evolved from obsessive tales like *From Her to Eternity* to the devotion of *Into My Arms*. The 2016 death of his teenage son Arthur became a catalyst for even deeper transformation, leading to works like *Skeleton Tree* and *Ghosteen*. His later music explores grief, spirituality and resilience with extraordinary grace.

Cave's *Red Hand Files*, his online letters to fans, also reveal a man who has integrated his past's darkness into a hard-won capacity for empathy and reflection.

What initially appears as the abandonment of an old self instead represents a deeper integration of both dark and light tendencies. Cave's journey illustrates that rather than rejecting our past, we can weave together our various lives into a more complete understanding of human experience. Here, early chaos and later wisdom are not opposed, but form a continuous thread of authentic *becoming*. The fury and intensity that once fuelled Cave's excess now powers his search for meaning and connection, suggesting that our Shadows, when acknowledged, can become a source of depth rather than destruction.

This is an approach to life that embraces uncertainty and questions our cultural obsession with predetermined routes to success. The Taoists of ancient China understood this conundrum, speaking of the way that cannot be named and the path that appears only by walking it. In *The Pathless Path*, strategy consultant Paul Millerd describes how leaving the traditional career track opened him to a more authentic way of living. This is one where meaning emerges through exploration rather than following prescribed steps. The pathless path requires courage precisely because it offers no guarantees, no markers of progress, no external validation that we are moving in the 'right' direction.

But how many of us cling to a single narrative of success or fulfilment, refusing to acknowledge other possibilities? What versions of ourselves do we dismiss because they do not fit our carefully constructed self-image? The journey toward authenticity often requires us to embrace uncertainty and question our most deeply held assumptions about who we are and what we are meant to become.

These ideas are central to Virginia Woolf's thesis in her book-length essay *A Room of One's Own*. Through the example of her fictional character Judith Shakespeare, Woolf examines how societal pressures can constrain the expression of our true potential. Judith shares the gifts of her playwright brother William, but she is not permitted in 1920s England to develop or express them because of her gender. She feels trapped by what others expect of her.

How many of our lives similarly are governed not by explicit prohibition but by subtle societal pressures, internalised limitations or unquestioned assumptions about what is acceptable or what constitutes success? What qualities do we suppress in pursuit of what others deem acceptable? How do these unlived lives – the careers we opt not to pursue, the talents we leave unexplored, the relationships we neglect to nurture – inform the lives we do lead?

UNLIVED LIVES

Our preoccupation with the lives we have not led reveals a fundamental aspect of human consciousness. In his book *On Not Being Someone Else*, the academic Andrew Miller explores how we use cultural artefacts like novels and films to address the persistent Shadows of alternative possibilities. These works serve as mirrors, reflecting our own curiosity about different paths, different choices, different selves. By engaging with narratives of unlived possibilities, we can explore the boundaries of our lives while finding meaning in them. Art animates ideas, and engaging with it brings us closer to understanding.

Akira Kurosawa's film *Ikiru*, for example, prompts the viewer to acknowledge the Shadow side of modern work itself. In the movie's first act, we see government clerk Kanji Watanabe (Takashi Shimura) mired in a soul-destroying, bureaucratic machine where he has spent thirty years stamping papers and conforming to meaningless procedure. Human vitality and purpose are sacrificed in deference to organisational efficiency that fails to meet the needs of the citizens the local government officials are meant to serve. The film touches on the universal truths of the capitalist system.

It can be argued that the modern workplace intensifies the tension between lived and unlived possibilities. In *Work, Self and Society*, business professor Catherine Casey illustrates how modern corporate culture systematically removes alternative ways of being. "The new corporatization of the self is more than a process of assault, discipline and defeat against which employees defend themselves," she argues. "It is a process of colonization in which, in its completion, *assault and defeat are no longer recognised.*" Workers not only abandon alternative life possibilities but lose the ability to conceive of them altogether.

In this way, Watanabe's conformity represents not just a personal choice but a systemic reshaping of the self, where overt displays of employee resistance and opposition are virtually eliminated, and the capacity for imagining different modes of work and being becomes increasingly constrained. However, when Watanabe is given a terminal stomach cancer diagnosis, it motivates him to confront both his mortality and the Shadow of his unlived life. To give meaning to his remaining months, Watanabe commits to genuine service and human connection. He dedicates himself to a community project, using his knowledge of local government systems to navigate the usual bureaucratic hurdles and unite disparate departments in the construction of a children's playground.

The psychotherapist Connie Zweig provides valuable insight into this territory of unlived potential, particularly through her analysis in *The Inner Work of Age* of how different life stages interact with our Shadow aspects. In early adulthood, Zweig argues, we often make choices that subordinate certain authentic parts of ourselves to meet external demands and expectations. We choose careers for security rather than passion, abandoning creative pursuits in favour of practical concerns. During our middle years, these unlived possibilities can re-emerge as a source of restlessness or regret, giving rise to what is commonly known as a midlife crisis.

It is in later life, as is the case with Watanabe, that we have both the opportunity and the psychological maturity to fully confront our Shadows. Zweig explores how ageing often places these Shadows in sharper relief, making us more aware of paths not taken and dreams deferred. The retirement transition becomes a pivotal juncture where unlived lives demand attention as we again consider our creative aspirations, call to service and the entrepreneurial ventures that we previously set aside.

Rather than a cause for regret, this presents an opportunity for reviewing our lives, and surfacing, examining and integrating dormant aspects of ourselves in ways that accommodate our current life stage. While we cannot enact every unlived possibility, we can acknowledge and honour these Shadows, enriching the remainder of our lives. For instance, this can be through community service, or teaching or mentoring the next generation.

In my own case, I applied to be a school teacher on three separate occasions and was accepted for a Postgraduate Certification at the University of Cambridge. I kept deferring because I felt the profession was poorly paid and subject to immense political interference. Upon honest reflection, I could see that my values at the time were driven more by money and conventional notions of achievement than by a desire for fulfilment. Today, I feel some sadness about this and wonder what it would have been like to have been a great teacher impacting the lives of young people.

Nevertheless, I now understand that I have been able to bring to life that yearning to teach in a different way, as a facilitator and speaker working with adults. It is not too late to reclaim the desire I once had. Today, there are organisations like Teach Now that allow late-career professionals to retrain and teach in inner-city schools. Their commercial and business experience can add something valuable that other teachers early in their careers may lack.

As Zweig's research suggests, unlived lives remain vital aspects of our psyches that continue to seek expression and integration. We carry them with us wherever we go. This notion is central to our understanding of Celine Song's film *Past Lives*. The viewer observes the choices made and the 'what if' paths not followed by the protagonists, Nora (Greta Lee) and Hae Sung (Teo Yoo). The childhood sweethearts lose contact with one another when Sung's family emigrates to Canada, and reconnect online when she moves to New York as an adult. Decisions about where each of them lives, the careers they pursue and the relationships they have all imply unfulfilled alternatives. The Shadows do not simply disappear. Instead, they persist as traces of possibility, shaping the protagonists' lives even through their absence.

While *Past Lives* explores the haunting quality of roads not taken, Wim Wenders's film *Perfect Days* offers a different perspective on how we might relate to these Shadow aspects of ourselves. The story of Hirayama (Kōji Yakusho) offers a striking counterpoint to conventional narratives about unlived lives. As a public toilet cleaner in Tokyo, Hirayama embodies what many would think of as a Shadow career, taking on the kind of work that ambitious professionals relegate to their unlived lives when dreaming of simplicity and direct service. His estranged sister Keijo (Yumi Asō) clearly looks down on what Hirayama does for a living. Her own wealth and status set her apart from her brother in a hierarchical societal system that she upholds and he disregards.

Yet, through the careful attention to the work he does, along with his appreciation of literature and music and engagement with the natural world, Hirayama reveals a life of remarkable richness and presence. His daily routines, far from representing a compromise or retreat from the so-called real world, show how our Shadows can be integrated into any form of work. He is an example of how our Shadow lives can enhance the lives we lead rather than causing us to abandon the paths we already follow.

In a world of busyness and efficiency, we too often dismiss qualities like attention to detail, physical engagement, slowness and direct human connection as impractical or unprofessional. *Perfect Days* suggests that these might be exactly what we need in order to navigate our rapidly changing world with wisdom and grace. As AI transforms the workplace, these Shadow elements take on new significance. They remind us of essential human qualities that no machine can replicate, including the capacity for presence, the wisdom of the body and the ability to find meaning in simple tasks well done.

This presence that Hirayama embodies represents something profound about Shadow Work itself. It is not about eliminating our Shadows or even fully resolving them, but rather maintaining awareness of them. When we lose this awareness, we become trapped in egoic dramas, projecting our unacknowledged aspects onto others, engaging in scapegoating and defensiveness. This disconnection from presence can lead to the very violence that composer Michael Tippett warned against, a form of spiritual bypassing that comes from refusing to confront our whole selves.

As Saint Irenaeus, the Greek Bishop, wrote, "The glory of God is a man fully alive." This vitality comes not from perfection but from complete acceptance. It is like standing naked in the rain, feeling everything, both pleasant and uncomfortable. This is the true promise of Shadow Work – not the elimination of our complexity, but the embrace of it. Through this acceptance comes genuine self-compassion and, by extension, compassion for others. We recognise that we are both intrinsically whole and indivisibly connected to each other.

The journey of Shadow Work is ultimately about acceptance, not perfection. It requires persistent curiosity about ourselves, particularly those aspects we find uncomfortable or inconvenient to examine. Just as the Buddha's father tried to shield him from life's complexities, our society serves up endless distractions, including advertising, social media, fast food, entertainment and the promise of quick fixes. But there is no bypassing this essential inner work. It is a journey each of us must make toward mature leadership and authentic living in these challenging times.

LEADERSHIP

The integration of our Shadows becomes particularly important in the context of leadership, where the pressure to maintain a carefully curated image often drives essential qualities underground. With AI already performing more of the procedural and analytical aspects of management, we must question what the uniquely human essence of leadership is. The answer may lie not in qualities like strategic brilliance, decisiveness and charismatic authority that we have traditionally celebrated in leaders, but in what has been cast into the Shadows.

Every leadership style, whether commanding, democratic, pacesetting, coaching or affiliative, has its own distinctive Shadow. A commanding leader's strength and decisiveness may create clarity, but their Shadow manifests as fear and compliance. A democratic leader's inclusiveness can foster engagement while creating a Shadow of indecision and endless deliberation. These Shadows inform not just individual interactions but ripple outward, influencing how teams function, and when they come from the top they can define organisational culture.

The first step in effective leadership is developing awareness of how our preferred style shapes the emotional and psychological environment around us. Research by psychologist Kurt Lewin and his colleagues shows how distinct leadership behaviours create markedly different organisational climates. These range from the authoritarian culture, which drives short-term results but stifles innovation, to the participative one, which builds commitment but may lack urgency. Understanding this requires us to look beyond the surface benefits of our natural style, recognising its hidden costs and unintended consequences.

The continued failure of traditional business education to prepare leaders for complex systemic challenges is difficult to ignore, as evidenced by the global financial crisis that began in 2007, haphazard management of the Covid pandemic and the generally tepid response to climate change. This reflects a deeper pattern in Western thought, where leadership is treated as a noun (a set of fixed attributes or positions) rather than as a verb that describes dynamic processes of influence and transformation. This mechanistic approach remains deeply rooted in masculine and industrial age paradigms and fails to address today's wicked problems.

Traditional leadership theory has emphasised visible, measurable qualities while relegating other capacities to the Shadows. In *The Culture of the New Capitalism*, sociologist Richard Sennett describes how the institutional culture this gives rise to prioritises immediate flexibility and change while eroding long-term commitment, loyalty and trust. The model pushes into the Shadows both what it overlooks and what it actively suppresses, including emotional intelligence, vulnerability and the capacity for genuine human connection.

Economist Kate Raworth elaborates on this in *Doughnut Economics*, arguing that contemporary organisations must shift from extraction and control toward regeneration and emergence, operating within planetary boundaries while ensuring social equity. This challenge requires a complete reimagining of leadership for a world of increasing complexity and interconnection.

Both *Ikiru* and *Perfect Days* provide examples of leadership that go beyond conventional practices. Watanabe's transformation in *Ikiru* illustrates what emergence from the Shadows might look like. He shifts from bureaucratic management to purposeful leadership, exhibiting moral courage and emotional authenticity, while catalysing systemic change. Hirayama's quiet leadership in *Perfect Days* also shows how presence and attention can inspire more effectively than traditional forms of authority.

These examples resonate with business school lecturer Otto Scharmer's *Theory U*, suggesting that the integration of leadership Shadows requires moving through denial and fear to reach a state of 'presencing.' This is a quality of attention and awareness that connects us to our deepest capacity for sensing and shaping the future. This type of journey becomes even more pertinent as AI transforms our organisations, requiring leaders to navigate not just technical changes but what the educators Ronald Heifetz and Marty Linsky refer to as adaptive challenges. These are problems that require changes in values, beliefs and ways of working.

Consider the intelligence displayed in Hirayama's work in *Perfect Days*, including his embodied knowledge of physical tasks, aesthetic sensitivity to light and shade, and emotional sensitivity to space and its meaning. These forms of intelligence, often dismissed simplistically as manual skill or intuition, represent Shadow capabilities that AI cannot easily imitate. They suggest ways of knowing that emerge from direct physical engagement with the world.

Emotional intelligence takes on new significance given the need for leaders to navigate complex emotional landscapes, read what is unspoken, sense and respond to human needs. But despite its importance, it has been relegated to the Shadows because of how we continue to privilege analytical thinking in other people and in the machine intelligence we have developed. This becomes even more striking when we acknowledge that global organisations like the World Economic Forum consistently identify human-centric skills as necessary for future workforce success. While technical competencies matter, capabilities relating to emotional awareness, relationship building and social understanding are vital and need to be integrated from the Shadows.

Mary Barra's leadership of General Motors offers a useful example. Barra transformed GM's approach to crisis management and innovation by combining technical expertise gained from her engineering background with remarkable emotional intelligence. Her handling of a mass recall of some 2.6 million cars due to a deadly mechanical flaw in 2014 spotlighted this dual capability. Barra displayed a technical grasp of complex safety issues while also expressing genuine empathy for affected customers and their families. This approach carried through to GM's electric vehicle transformation, where she balanced bold technical vision with careful attention to workforce concerns and customer relationships.

The future of leadership lies not in competing with what AI and other technologies can accomplish, but in nurturing those uniquely human capacities that currently lie in the Shadows. Leaders need to model authentic engagement with both the light and dark tendencies of organisational life, integrating them to help create life-enhancing, ecologically sustainable organisations. This path requires embracing leadership as a dynamic, embodied practice that engages with the full spectrum of what it means to be human.

SUCCESS

As we navigate an era of unprecedented change and complexity, we must reconsider our relationship with success and achievement. The conventional narrative of success, encompassing measurable accomplishments, wealth accumulation and status, has shown its limitations, revealing a Shadow side that affects both individuals and society. This Shadow manifests when we attain our stated goals without any sense of achievement, sacrifice our authentic selves in pursuit of external validation, or our drive for success exacts hidden costs on our well-being, relationships and the environment.

Within what philosopher Byung-Chul Han refers to as the *achievement society*, success occupies a central role, with intricate systems in place to measure, quantify and display it. These range from performance metrics to social media likes, quarterly profits to hierarchical status and asset inventories to career trajectories. However, our pursuit of these visible markers of success has obscured other forms of achievement and meaning, each carrying its own Shadow aspects that we must learn to recognise and integrate.

The beliefs we hold about success and life itself shape our journey. Some view life as a brief opportunity for pleasure and accumulation of experiences and possessions. Others see it as a quest for meaning and fulfilment. Still others frame it through the lens of achievements and accolades, while some reject what they perceive as life's endless rat race. Each of these perspectives carries its own Shadows, in terms of both their gifts and limitations. The hedonist might find short-term pleasure but lack deeper fulfilment, while those solely focused on *meaning* might need to 'live a little' and embrace joy. The high achiever may collect accolades yet feel hollow, while those who drop out might grapple with listlessness and spiritual sloth.

The Shadow of success reveals itself in the stories of those who reached the pinnacle of conventional achievement only to find themselves struggling with emptiness and addiction. Actor Matthew Perry's memoir, *Friends, Lovers, and the Big Terrible Thing*, poignantly illustrates this paradox. Despite gaining wealth, fame and all the material trappings he had dreamed of, Perry found himself trapped in a cycle of addiction, searching for meaning beyond his achievements. Although he had reportedly been clean in his final months, Perry's life ended tragically in 2023 when he drowned in his Los Angeles hot tub following a ketamine overdose. His story serves as a complex reminder that even those who successfully battle their demons remain vulnerable to success's Shadow side, and that the path to healing is rarely straightforward.

Former Lloyds Bank CEO António Horta-Osório's very public burnout in 2011 also highlights how even the most accomplished executives are not immune to the crushing pressure of achievement culture. After reaching the top of the banking world, Horta-Osório needed to step back and seek professional help for severe insomnia and exhaustion. As is noted in the *Tao Te Ching*, the ancient Taoist philosophical treatise, "Success is as dangerous as failure ... Whether you go up the ladder or down it, your position is shaky." True stability comes not from our position on the ladder but from staying grounded in our authentic selves.

These individual struggles play out within larger organisational and societal structures that have their own Shadow systems. Beyond the formal hierarchies and stated values lie unofficial networks, unwritten rules, unspoken power relationships and implicit agreements that influence how success is defined, measured and pursued. These organisational Shadows often become most visible during periods of change, when established patterns are disrupted and what lurks in the collective unconscious rises to the surface.

In approaching these Shadow systems, the goal is not to eliminate them entirely or expose every hidden pattern. Rather, success lies in developing a more sophisticated understanding of organisational complexity itself. By acknowledging these deeper layers instead of trying to suppress them, we create space for new definitions of achievement to emerge, ones that align more closely with human purpose and moral courage. This integration of light and dark tendencies, rather than the triumph of one over the other, becomes crucial for sustainable organisational transformation in an increasingly uncertain world.

Our modern economic system exemplifies this interplay of light and darkness. While capitalism has generated unprecedented prosperity and innovation, driving technological advancement and raising living standards for many around the globe, it also has created profound unintended consequences. As Raworth argues, traditional economic thinking has systematically externalised costs, pushing the true financial and environmental burden of production and consumption on to society, the natural world and future generations. These Shadows manifest in environmental degradation, social inequality and psychological distress.

Perhaps most insidiously, market logic has colonised even our inner lives, transforming rest and reflection into opportunities for quantification and optimisation. What was once sacred personal time has become another arena for self-improvement and productivity tracking. Meditation apps gamify mindfulness, sleep trackers score our rest and wellness programmes turn self-care into a metric to be measured. This commodification of contemplation reflects a deeper paradox. In our pursuit of optimisation, we risk losing touch with the very qualities – presence, spontaneity, genuine reflection – that make us human.

At the heart of this commodification lies a fundamental shift in our relationship with time. Unlike our ancestors, today we prioritise speed, immediacy and productivity to the detriment of the slowness, reflection and fallow periods enjoyed by Hirayama in *Perfect Days*. According to Han, we have lost the capacity for deep attention, replacing it with hyperactive yet shallow forms of engagement.

Encouragingly, many now acknowledge that there are alternative paths that can be followed. Some people already pursue interests and passions that exist alongside their primary work, in the form of a 'side gig' Shadow career. Others, as author Paul Millerd suggests in *Good Work*, seek to integrate personal values and interests in their professional lives, even when they diverge from the traditional measures of success. This trend is accelerating. Research by management consultancy Korn Ferry on talent acquisition trends for 2025 indicates that employers must evolve their Employee Value Propositions (EVPs) to attract talented people who prioritise purpose, flexibility and work-life integration over conventional career advancement.

With technological changes disrupting traditional career paths, many people are embracing a more adaptive, multifaceted approach. Roz Savage, for example, has been a record-breaking oceanic rower, management and leadership consultant, author and climate activist. She is now a Member of the Parliament in the U.K. By leveraging diverse skills and experiences, Savage has been able to find fulfilment and make meaningful contributions across multiple domains. As the job market continues to evolve, embracing this kind of versatility and following our own authentic interests may prove to be essential for personal well-being and professional longevity.

However, confronting the Shadow of success does not mean rejecting achievement or excellence. Rather, it involves expanding our understanding of what constitutes accomplishment. Success could entail passionate dedication to meaningful work, mindful attention to daily tasks and the cultivation of genuine human relationships. This integration of what has been in the Shadows into our definition of success could help us develop more sustainable and fulfilling ways of living and working.

We have an opportunity to redefine success in more nuanced and holistic ways. This is not about choosing between achievement and authenticity, or between growth and sustainability. Rather, it is about learning to navigate the full spectrum of success, integrating external accomplishments with internal fulfilment, technological advancement with human wisdom and individual achievement with collective well-being. This integration could point the way toward a healthier, more sustainable relationship with work and achievement. Such an approach honours both our pursuit of excellence and our need for meaning. Ultimately, though, we must remember that true stability comes not from our position on any ladder but from standing firmly in our whole selves.

INTEGRATION

The integration of Shadows in our working lives is not merely a philosophical exercise, but an urgent practical necessity. Integration aligns closely with what Jung termed *individuation*, the psychological process of integrating the conscious with the unconscious, leading to the realisation of the Self. Through this work, individuals can expect to experience greater authenticity, reduced internal conflict, enhanced creativity and deeper relationships. Organisations that support this integration often see improved innovation, stronger team performance and more sustainable success.

How do we move from understanding Shadow patterns to living more wholly integrated lives? How do we create organisations and societies that support rather than suppress this integration?

The path toward integration often begins with simple yet profound shifts in attention. Like Hirayama in *Perfect Days*, we might start by bringing fuller awareness to whatever task is at hand, regardless of its perceived status or importance. This practice of presence, of embodied attention, creates spaces where Shadows can emerge and be acknowledged. It suggests that integration is not always about dramatic transformation, but perhaps changing the quality of our engagement with what already exists.

Some might view the following proposals as utopian, reminiscent of economist John Maynard Keynes's 1930 prediction of a 15-hour workweek by 2030. But by building on this foundation of presence, we can explore how integration might manifest at the organisational and societal level. For example, Universal Basic Income (UBI) – the concept of a government programme that would provide every citizen with a regular, unconditional cash payment – has potential not only as an economic solution to poverty and inequality but as a tool for Shadow integration at a societal level. By providing basic financial security, UBI might enable people to engage more authentically with Shadow careers. It would allow them to pursue meaningful work regardless of its market value while integrating aspects of themselves that economic necessity previously had forced them to suppress.

Organisations play a vital role in this integration process. We need to create *holding spaces* where Shadow aspects can be safely explored and integrated by encouraging contact and dialogue with other people through environmental design. Leading companies have already begun experimenting with such spaces. Alphabet's Googleplex and Pixar's headquarters are designed specifically to encourage serendipitous encounters, creative play and embodied presence.

At the animation studio Pixar, for instance, the main bathrooms have been intentionally placed in the atrium to force people from different departments to cross paths and interact. These physical spaces support not just innovation but the integration of Shadow elements that might otherwise remain hidden. A studio artist, for example, might normally avoid interaction with financial managers, seeing them as representing the constraining, bureaucratic aspects they reject in themselves. But when forced to share space regularly, they might discover unexpected common ground. Perhaps the manager has creative interests, or the artist has a hidden talent for systemic thinking. The design of physical space actively brings Shadow elements into consciousness through their daily encounters.

Looking beyond the individual and organisational levels, we must also consider how to restructure work itself to better support integration. This could involve creating roles that combine functions that traditionally have been separated, developing evaluation systems that value Shadow capabilities and designing career paths that encourage Shadow exploration. For example, some organisations now include reverse-mentoring programmes where junior employees advise senior leaders on topics like technology or diversity, helping both parties confront their assumptions about hierarchy and knowledge.

Other organisations have evolved beyond traditional performance metrics. The e-commerce giant Alibaba, for instance, evaluates employees' emotional intelligence and capacity for relationships in addition to their technical skills. Outdoor apparel retailer Patagonia assess employees' contributions to the company's culture and environmental mission, recognising that sustainable business requires capabilities beyond conventional metrics. These skills and talents often are relegated to the Shadows in conventional business environments.

The process of integration requires new forms of conversation in our organisations and communities. We need ways to acknowledge and discuss our Shadows without sensationalising or diminishing them. This might look like the 'courageous conversations' programmes adopted by companies like Starbucks and Microsoft to discuss challenging topics like racial bias and systemic inequity. At investment firm Bridgewater Associates, the practice of radical transparency includes regular feedback sessions where employees at all levels are encouraged to voice concerns and critique decisions openly, including those aimed at senior leadership. These conversations are themselves integration practices, as they normalise the examination of what usually remains unspoken at work.

Yet, in our increasingly digital world, such conversations and integration efforts cannot be limited to physical spaces and face-to-face interactions. This raises important questions about technology's role in Shadow integration. How can we reimagine our use of technology from an integration perspective? Rather than using AI to replace human capabilities, can we design systems that enhance embodied presence and our relationship with all forms of intelligence, whether human or nonhuman?

How can technology improve how we work not only with each other and with machine intelligence, but with the intelligence of the natural world as well?

For instance, biofeedback devices could help us become more attuned to our body's subtle responses during difficult conversations, while virtual reality environments might create safe spaces for exploring Shadow aspects we typically avoid. Similarly, AI systems could be designed to notice and reflect our unconscious patterns – not to judge or correct them, but to increase our awareness and capacity for integration.

Cultural change is essential. Cultural anthropologist Catherine Bateson calls for developing the ability to notice and value what happens at the edges of our attention, in our cultural peripheral vision. This might involve creating new stories about success and meaning, devising new metrics for organisational and societal health, or finding new ways to acknowledge and reward Shadow capabilities. Companies like Supercell, the Finnish digital game developer, exemplify this approach. They celebrate failed projects with champagne, understanding that what lies in the Shadows of failure often contains the seeds of future success. Their post-mortem processes explicitly seek to extract learning from what did not work, bringing these Shadow aspects into the light of organisational consciousness.

The goal of integration is not to eliminate Shadows. As should be clear by now, they will always exist. But we do need to develop a conscious and healthy relationship with them. This requires an ongoing practice of attention, reflection and engagement. We must learn to work with Shadows as sources of wisdom and creativity rather than problems to be solved or feared.

The integration of Shadows is essential for both individual and collective well-being. Through the process of individuation, we can expect to experience both personal transformation and organisational and societal evolution. As we have seen, our Shadows are not merely personal psychological phenomena, but have significant implications for our organisations, our societies, and our relationships with technology and the natural world. By embracing the Shadows as a source of gifts as well as darkness, by recognising their collective as well as personal dimensions, and by approaching them as multifaceted rather than purely psychological, we can find a new path to a more integrated and holistic way of living and working. In this way, we can truly unlock our full potential.

TOUCHING THE EARTH

Let's return to the young Siddhartha, sheltered within his father's palace. What Shadows lurked at the edges of that manufactured paradise? Every servant instructed to hide signs of ageing, every guard posted to keep death and illness at bay, every entertainment designed to distract from life's deeper questions created an intricate system of Shadow management that would eventually crack under its own weight.

When Siddhartha finally encountered what had been hidden, he did not simply exchange one extreme for another. His journey was not just from pleasure to asceticism, from privilege to renunciation. Instead, he moved toward integration, toward what would become known as the Middle Way. This path required him to face not only the Shadows his father had hidden but also the Shadows of his own making.

The Buddha's enlightenment under the Bodhi tree represents a powerful example of Shadow integration. In that moment, faced with the demon Mara's temptations and threats, which were intended to prevent Siddhartha from achieving enlightenment, he did not banish the interloper, but instead touched the earth. In doing this, he acknowledges his connection to all of existence, in both its darkness and its light. The Buddha's gesture of acceptance offers a model for our own integration work.

Today's equivalent of King Śuddhodana's palace might be found in our carefully curated social media feeds, in corporate wellness programmes that promote positivity while ignoring systemic issues, in AI systems designed to shield us from uncertainty and complexity. Like the palace guards who cleared away signs of suffering, our modern systems often work to hide what makes us uncomfortable.

Yet, as both Watanabe and Hirayama demonstrate in their different ways, authentic integration often begins with simply turning toward what we have been conditioned to avoid. Watanabe faces not only his mortality but the mechanical nature of his bureaucratic existence. Hirayama embraces work that many would believe was beneath them, finding in it a source of dignity and presence. Both men, in their way, touch the earth as the Buddha did, acknowledging their connection to all aspects of existence.

The integration of Shadows does not promise enlightenment in the Buddhist sense. But it does offer the possibility of a more authentic way of being, one that embraces the full spectrum of human experience. This integration manifests differently for each of us. For some, it might mean acknowledging creative aspirations that have long been suppressed. For others, it could involve embracing leadership capabilities that we have denied. Or, it might mean reconnecting with simple physical tasks or natural rhythms that we have forgotten.

What unites these various paths is the willingness to turn toward, rather than away from, our Shadows. This pivot requires presence, including the kind of attention Hirayama brings to his daily tasks, the moral courage Watanabe discovers in his final months, and the awareness that allows us to notice what lies at the edges of our carefully constructed lives.

The Buddha's example suggests that this integration work is never finished. Even after his enlightenment, he spent 45 years teaching, adapting his message to different audiences, working with the Shadows of confusion, resistance and attachment in his students. Similarly, our own integration work is ongoing. It requires us to repeatedly turn toward what we would rather avoid, acknowledge what we would rather deny, embrace what we would rather reject.

Living the Shadow Life entails neither running from nor chasing after our Shadows, but learning to dance with them. It means developing the capacity to move fluidly between light and dark, between knowing and not knowing, between doing and being. This dance requires both the courage to face what we have avoided and the humility to acknowledge that our Shadows will always be with us.

In this dance, we might find not just personal integration but new possibilities for collective transformation. As we learn to work with our own Shadows, we can develop the capacity to help others work with theirs. As we integrate our own unlived lives, we can create space for new forms of organisation and society to emerge.

The journey that began with Siddhartha's departure from his father's palace continues in each of us as we face our own Shadows, integrate our unlived lives and discover what lies beyond the palace walls. Through this exploratory journey, I have come to learn that the ongoing work of integration – personal and collective, individual and systemic – might be our most important task in an age of unprecedented change and challenge.

SHADOW REFLECTIONS

- Reflect on the some of the most pivotal decisions of your life. What informed these choices, internal desires or external expectations? Can you identify the deeper desires and patterns underlying these decisions?

- What unlived life do you grieve? How do your regrets impact your present experience?

- How might you find deeper meaning in the ordinary moments of your life?

- How would you describe your leadership style? How has this been shaped, and what distinctly human capabilities do you want to develop and lead with?

- What environment do you create for those you lead? Is it one of safety and empowerment, or a place of anxiety and confusion?

- How has your definition of success evolved? If success were a process rather than an end goal, how would you reimagine it?

- How might you embrace technologies like AI to enhance your leadership while preserving your natural human capabilities?

- What have you learned about your Shadows through this exploration? How has your relationship with yourself and others shifted as a result?

- What does 'touching the earth' and dancing with your Shadows mean to you? How might you journey further beyond 'the palace walls' of this book and further explore your Shadows?

BIBLIOGRAPHY

Abbs-Street, Annabel. *Sleepless: Unleashing the Subversive Power of the Night Self.* Putnam, 2024.

Akomolafe, Bayo. *These Wilds Beyond Our Fences: Letters to My Daughter on Humanity's Search for Home.* North Atlantic Books, 2017.

Akomolafe, Bayo. 'When You Meet the Monster, Anoint Its Feet', *Emergence Magazine,* 16 October 2018. https://emergencemagazine. org/essay/when-you-meet-the-monster/.

Argyris, Chris. *Overcoming Organisational Defenses: Facilitating Organisational Learning.* Allyn and Bacon, 1990.

Askenberger, Ann. *A 12-Point Guide to Constructing a Modern Honey-Ghost-Trap: A Leadership-Development Process for Increasing Self Awareness.* Insead, Executive Master in Change Thesis, 2021. https://flora.insead.edu/fichiersti_wp/inseademctheseswave30/97910.pdf.

Askenberger, Ann. *Your Shadow Is Your Strength: The Power of Embracing the Hidden Sides Within You in Your Leadership.* Erlanders, 2023.

Barrett, Laurence. *A Jungian Approach to Coaching: The Theory and Practice of Turning Leaders into People.* Routledge, 2023.

Bateson, Gregory. *Steps to an Ecology of Mind: Collected Essays in Anthropology, Psychiatry, Evolution, and Epistemology.* Jason Aronson, 1987.

Bateson, Mary Catherine. *Peripheral Visions: Learning Along the Way.* HarperCollins, 1994.

Beaton, Connor. *Shadow Course*. Modules 1–8. Course materials distributed to participants in 2024. https://mantalks.com/shadow-course/.

Belfort, Jordan. *Catching the Wolf of Wall Street*. Bantam Books, 2009.

Belfort, Jordan. *The Wolf of Wall Street*. Bantam Books, 2007.

Bendell, Jem. *Breaking Together: A Freedom-Loving Response to Collapse*. Good Works, 2023.

Berne, Eric. *Games People Play: The Psychology of Human Relationships*. Penguin, 1973.

Berry-Hillman, Patricia. 'The Training of the Shadow and the Shadow of the Training', *Journal of Analytical Psychology*, 26(3), 1981.

Blakely, Grace. *Vulture Capitalism: Corporate Crimes, Backdoor Bailouts and the Death of Freedom*. Bloomsbury, 2024.

Bly, Robert. *A Little Book on the Human Shadow*. HarperCollins, 2009. Edited by William Booth.

Bolte Taylor, Jill. *My Stroke of Insight*. Hodder & Stoughton, 2009.

Bouchard, Gérard. *Social Myths and Collective Imaginaries*. University of Toronto Press, 2017. Translated by Howard Scott.

Briers, Francis. 'Embodied Leadership', *Training Journal*, December 2015. https://www.trainingjournal.com/2016/uncategorised/embodied-leadership/.

Brooks, David. *The Social Animal: The Hidden Sources of Love, Character, and Achievement*. Random House, 2011.

Brown, Brené. *Atlas of the Heart: Mapping Meaningful Connection and the Language of Human Experience*. Random House, 2021.

Brulé, Dan. *Just Breathe: Mastering Breathwork for Success in Life, Love, Business, and Beyond*. Enliven Books. 2017.

Burgis, Luke. *Wanting: The Power of Mimetic Desire in Everyday Life*. St Martin's Press, 2021.

Burkus, David. *Best Team Ever: The Surprising Science of High-Performing Teams*. Twinbolt, 2023.

Burkus, David. *Friend of a Friend: Understanding the Hidden Networks That Can Transform Your Life and Career*. Houghton Mifflin Harcourt, 2018.

Casey, Catherine. *Work, Self and Society: After Industrialism*. Routledge, 1995.

Catto, Jamie. *Insanely Gifted: Turn Your Demons into Creative Rocket Fuel*. Canongate, 2016.

Centre of Applied Jungian Studies. *Magnum Opus Nigredo*. Modules 1–6. Course materials distributed to participants in 2023-24. https://appliedjung.com/nigredo/.

Chamorro-Premuzic, Tomas. 'Could Your Personality Derail Your Career?', *Harvard Business Review*, September–October 2017. https://hbr.org/2017/09/could-your-personality-derail-your-career.

Chamorro-Premuzic, Tomas. *I, Human: AI, Automation, and the Quest to Reclaim What Makes Us Unique*. Harvard Business Review Press, 2023.

Chamorro-Premuzic, Tomas. 'Should You Bring Your Whole Self to Work?', *Forbes*, 2 June 2020. https://www.forbes.com/sites/tomaspremuzic/2020/06/02/should-you-bring-your-whole-self-to-work/.

Chamorro-Premuzic, Tomas. 'Why Do So Many Incompetent Men Become Leaders?', *Harvard Business Review*, 23 August 2013. https://hbr.org/2013/08/why-do-so-many-incompetent-men.

Chatterjee, Rangan. *Make Change That Lasts: 9 Simple Ways to Break Free from the Habits that Hold Your Back*. Penguin Life, 2025.

Chesnut, Robert, with Joan O'C. Hamilton. *Intentional Integrity: How Smart Companies Can Lead An Ethical Revolution*. St. Martin's Press, 2020.

Chödrön, Pema, *When Things Fall Apart: Heart Advice for Difficult Times*. Shambhala Publications, 2000.

Cohen, Andrew, with Hans Plasqui. *When Shadow Meets the Bodhisattva: The Challenging Transformation of a Modern Guru*. Inner Traditions, 2023.

Cohn, Ruth. 'The Shape of Shame: Trauma, Posture and Coming to Tall', *Ruth Cohn: Neglect-Informed Psychotherapy*, no date. https://ruthcohnmft.com/on-my-mind/the-shape-of-shame-trauma-posture-and-coming-to-tall/.

Csikszentmihalyi, Mihaly. *The Evolving Self: A Psychology for the Third Millennium*. HarperPerennial, 1994.

Damasio, Antonio. *Descartes' Error: Emotion, Reason, and the Human Brain*. Penguin, 2005.

Damasio, Antonio. *Feeling and Knowing: Making Minds Conscious*. Pantheon Books, 2021.

Davies, Dan. *The Unaccountability Machine: Why Big Systems Make Terrible Decisions – and How the World Lost Its Mind.* Profile Books, 2024.

de Botton, Alain. *A Therapeutic Journey: Lessons from The School of Life.* The School of Life, 2023.

Dederer, Claire. *Monsters: What Do We Do with Great Art by Bad People?* Sceptre, 2023.

De Haan, Erik, and Anthony Kasozi. *The Leadership Shadow: How to Recognize and Avoid Derailment, Hubris and Overdrive.* Kogan Page, 2014.

Demartini, John F. *The Breakthrough Experience: A Revolutionary New Approach to Personal Transformation.* Hay House, 2002.

Dilts, Robert. *Changing Belief Systems with NLP.* Meta Publications, 1990.

Durvasula, Ramani. *'Don't You Know Who I Am?' How to Stay Sane in an Era of Narcissism, Entitlement, and Incivility.* Post Hill Press, 2019.

Durvasula, Ramani. *It's Not You: Identifying and Healing from Narcissistic People.* The Open Field / Penguin Life, 2024.

Edmondson, Amy. *The Fearless Organisation: Creating Psychological Safety in the Workplace for Learning Innovation and Growth.* Wiley, 2019.

Edmondson, Amy. *Right Kind of Wrong: The Science of Failing Well.* Atria Books, 2023.

Edwards, Betty. *Drawing on the Right Side of the Brain: A Course in Enhancing Creativity and Artistic Confidence.* Souvenir Press, 2013, fourth edition.

Ekman, Paul. *Emotions Revealed: Understanding Faces and Feelings.* Weidenfeld & Nicolson, 2004.

Elliott, Carolyn. *Existential Kink: Unmask Your Shadow and Embrace Your Power.* Weiser Books, 2020.

English, Otto. *Fake Heroes: Ten False Icons and How They Altered the Course of History.* Headline Welbeck, 2024.

Fadiman, James, and Jordan Gruber. *Your Symphony of Selves: Discover and Understand More of Who We Are.* Park Street Press, 2020.

Fitzgerald, F. Scott. 'The Crack-Up', *Esquire*, February–April 1936. https://www.esquire.com/lifestyle/a4310/the-crack-up/.

Fox, Matthew. *The Reinvention of Work: A New Vision of Livelihood for Our Time.* HarperSanFrancisco. 1994.

Frankfurt, Harry. *On Bullshit*. Princeton University Press, 2005.

Geertz, Clifford. *The Interpretation of Cultures: Selected Essays.* Basic Books, 2017, third edition.

Girard, René. *The Scapegoat*. The Johns Hopkins University Press, 1986. Translated by Yvonne Freccero.

Girard, René. *Violence and the Sacred*. Bloomsbury Academic, 2013. Translated by Patrick Gregory.

Giridharadas, Anand. *Winners Take All: The Elite Charade of Changing the World*. Alfred A. Knopf, 2018.

Gloag, Kenneth. *Tippett: A Child of Our Time*. Cambridge University Press, 2010.

Goffee, Rob, and Gareth Jones. *The Character of a Corporation: How Your Company's Culture Can Make or Break Your Business*. Profile Books, 2003, second edition.

Grant, Adam. *Think Again: The Power of Knowing What You Don't Know*. Viking, 2021.

Hamilton, Diane Musho. *Everything is Workable: A Zen Approach to Conflict Resolution*. Shambhala Publications, 2013.

Han, Byung-Chul. *The Burnout Society*. Stanford Briefs, 2015. Translated by Erik Butler.

Hayashi, Arawana. *Social Presencing Theater: The Art of Making a True Move*. PI Press, 2021. https://www.u-school.org/spt.

Heider, John. *The Tao of Leadership*. Gower, 1993.

Heifetz, Ronald. *Leadership Without Easy Answers*. Belknap Press, 1994.

Heifetz, Ronald, and Marty Linsky. *Leadership on the Line: Staying Alive Through the Dangers of Change*. Harvard Business Review Press, 2017.

Heifetz, Ronald, Alexander Grashow and Marty Linsky. *The Practice of Adaptive Leadership: Tools and Tactics for Changing Your Organisation and the World*. Harvard Business Press, 2009.

Hendricks, Gay. *The Big Leap: A Guide to Transcending Personal Limits, Overcoming Fears, and Unleashing Your Authentic Greatness for a Better Life*. Harper One, 2010.

Highsmith, Patricia. *The Talented Mr Ripley.* Vintage, 1999.

Hildyard, Daisy. *The Second Body.* Fitzcarraldo Editions, 2017.

Hillman, James. *Uniform Edition of the Writings of James Hillman, Volume 1: Archetypal Psychology.* Spring Publications, 2015.

Hillman, Laurence, and Richard Olivier. *Archetypes at Work: Evolving Your Story, One Character at a Time.* Matador, 2019.

Hogan, Robert, Robert B. Kaiser, Ryne A. Sherman and Peter D. Harms. 'Twenty Years on the Dark Side: Six Lessons About Bad Leadership', *Consulting Psychology Journal: Practice and Research*, 73(3), July 2021.

Housel, Morgan. *The Psychology of Money: Timeless Lessons on Wealth, Greed, and Happiness.* Harriman House, 2020.

Hyde, Lewis. *Trickster Makes This World: How Disruptive Imagination Creates Culture.* Canongate, 2008.

Ibarra, Herminia. *Working Identity: Unconventional Strategies for Reinventing Your Career.* Harvard Business School Press, 2004.

Isaacson, Walter. *Steve Jobs: The Exclusive Biography.* Abacus, 2011.

Jackson, Rosemary. *Fantasy: The Literature of Subversion.* Routledge, 2009.

Johnson, Barry. *Polarity Management: Identifying and Managing Unsolvable Problems.* HRD Press, 1996.

Johnson, Robert A. *Your Own Shadow: Understanding the Dark Side of the Psyche.* HarperOne, 1993.

Jung, C. G. *The Collected Works of C. G. Jung, Volumes 1–19.* Princeton University Press, 2014, complete digital edition. Edited and translated by Gerhard Adler and R. F. C. Hull.

Kahneman, Daniel. *Thinking, Fast and Slow.* Penguin, 2012.

Kapuściński, Ryszard. *The Other.* Verso, 2018. Translated by Antonia Lloyd-Jones.

Kashdan, Todd, and Robert Biswas-Diener. *The Upside of Your Dark Side: Why Being Your Whole Self—Not Just Your 'Good' Self—Drives Success and Fulfillment.* Hudson Street Press, 2014.

Katie, Byron. *Loving What Is: Four Questions That Can Change Your Life.* Rider, 2002.

Kegan, Robert, and Lisa Laskow Lahey. *Immunity to Change: How to Overcome It and Unlock the Potential in Yourself and Your Organisation.* Harvard Business Press, 2009.

Kenny, Kate. *Whistleblowing: Toward a New Theory.* Harvard University Press, 2019.

Kets de Vries, Manfred F. R. *Down the Rabbit Hole of Leadership: Leadership Pathology in Everyday Life.* Palgrave Macmillan, 2019.

Klaas, Brian. *Corruptible: Who Gets Power and How It Changes Us.* Scribner, 2021.

Kenny, Kate. *Whistleblowing: Toward a New Theory.* Harvard University Press, 2019.

Klein, Melanie. *Envy and Gratitude and Other Works, 1946-1963.* Vintage Classics, 1997.

Klein, Naomi. *Doppelganger: A Trip into the Mirror World.* Farrar, Strauss and Giroux, 2023.

Klontz, Brad, Sonya L. Britt, Jennifer Mentzer and Ted Klontz. 'Money Beliefs and Financial Behaviors: Development of the Klontz Money Script Inventory', *The Journal of Financial Theory*, volume 2, issue 1, 2011. https://caas.usu.edu/fcse/files/money-beliefs-and-financial-behaviors-development-the-klontz-money-script-inventory-jft-2011.pdf.

Koenig, John. *The Dictionary of Obscure Sorrows.* Simon & Schuster, 2021. https://www.thedictionaryofobscuresorrows.com/.

Kopp, Sheldon B. *If You Meet Buddha on the Road, Kill Him! The Pilgrimage of Psychotherapy Patients.* Bantam, 1976.

Lacan, Jacques. *Écrits: A Selection.* Routledge, 1989. Translated by Alan Sheridan.

Landsberg, Max. *The Power of the Dao: Seven Essential Habits for Living in Flow, Fulfilment and Resilience.* LID Publishing, 2023.

Le Guin, Ursula K. 'The Child and the Shadow', *The Quarterly Journal of the Library of Congress,* 32(2), April 1975.

Lembke, Anna. *Dopamine Nation: Why Our Addiction to Pleasure Is Causing Us Pain*. Headline, 2023.

Lewin, Kurt, Ronald Lippitt and Ralph K. White. 'Patterns of Aggressive Behavior in Experimentally Created "Social Climates"', *The Journal of Social Psychology*, 10, 1939.

Lighthorse, Pixie. *Goldmining the Shadows: Honoring the Medicine of Wounds*. Row House Publishing, 2022.

Lindelblad, Björn Natthiko, Caroline Bankler and Navid Modiri. *I May Be Wrong: And Other Wisdoms from Life as a Forest Monk*. Bloomsbury, 2022.

Low, James. *Finding Freedom: Texts from the Theravadin, Mahayana and Dzogchen Buddhist Traditions*. Wandel Verlag / Edition Khordong, 2019. Introduced and translated by James Low.

Lukianoff, Greg, and Jonathan Haidt. *The Coddling of the American Mind: How Good Intentions and Bad Ideas Are Setting Up a Generation for Failure*. Penguin, 2018.

Lukianoff, Greg, and Rikki Schlott. *The Canceling of the American Mind: Cancel Culture Undermines Trust and Threatens Us All—But There is a Solution*. Simon & Schuster, 2023.

Lyth, Isabel Menzies. *Containing Anxieties in Institutions: Selected Essays, Volume 1*. Free Association Books, 1988.

Lyth, Isabel Menzies. *The Dynamics of the Social: Selected Essays, Volume 2*. Free Association Books, 1989.

Manning, Erin. *Relationscapes: Movement, Art, Philosophy*. MIT Press, 2009.

Manning, Erin. *The Minor Gesture*. Duke University Press, 2016.

Manning, Erin, and Brian Massumi. *Thought in the Act: Passages in the Ecology of Experience*. University of Minnesota Press, 2014.

Marshak, Robert J. *Covert Processes at Work: Managing the Hidden Dimensions of Organisational Change*. Berrett-Koehler Publishers, 2006.

Martin, Betty, with Robyn Dalzen. *The Art of Receiving and Giving: The Wheel of Consent*. Luminaire Press, 2021.

Maté, Gabor. *In the Realm of Hungry Ghosts: Close Encounters with Addiction*. Vermilion, 2018.

Maté, Gabor. *When the Body Says No: The Cost of Hidden Stress*. Scribe, 2019.

Maté, Gabor, with Daniel Maté. *The Myth of Normal: Trauma, Illness and Healing in a Toxic Culture*. Avery, 2022.

McGilchrist, Iain. *The Master and His Emissary: The Divided Brain and the Making of the Western World*. Yale University Press, 2019, expanded edition.

McGilchrist, Iain. *Ways of Attending: How Our Divided Brain Constructs the World*. Routledge, 2019.

Mclaughlin, Rosanna. *Double-Tracking: Studies in Duplicity*. Little Island Press / Carcanet, 2019.

Miller, Andrew H. *On Not Being Someone Else: Tales of Our Unled Lives*. Harvard University Press, 2020.

Miller, Christian B. *The Character Gap: How Good Are We?* Oxford University Press, 2018.

Millerd, Paul. *Good Work: Reclaiming Your Inner Ambition*. Pathless Publishing, 2024.

Millerd, Paul. *The Pathless Path: Imagining a New Story for Work and Life*. Pathless Publishing, 2022.

Monbiot, George, and Peter Hutchison. *The Invisible Doctrine: The Secret History of Neoliberalism (& How It Came to Control Your Life)*. Allen Lane, 2024.

Moore, Robert, and Douglas Gillette. *King, Warrior, Magician, Lover: Rediscovering the Archetypes of the Mature Masculine*. HarperSanFrancisco, 1991.

Nadella, Satya, with Greg Shaw and Jill Tracie Nichols. *Hit Refresh: The Quest to Rediscover Microsoft's Soul and Imagine a Better Future for Everyone*. Harper Business, 2017.

National Institute for the Clinical Application of Behavioral Medicine. *How to Work with the Shadow Side*. Modules 1–6. Course materials distributed to participants in 2024. https://www.nicabm.com/program/shadow-side-1.

Nesse, Randolph M. *Good Reasons for Bad Feelings: Insights from the Frontier of Evolutionary Psychiatry*. Dutton, 2019.

Neumann, Erich. *Depth Psychology and a New Ethic*. Shambhala, 1990. Translated by Eugene Rolfe.

Nin, Anaïs. *Seduction of the Minotaur.* Swallow Press, 2014, updated edition.

Nussbaum, Martha C. *The Monarchy of Fear: A Philosopher Looks at Our Political Crisis.* Oxford University Press, 2018.

Obama, Michelle. *Becoming.* Penguin, 2021.

Ohno, Kazuo, and Yoshito Ohno. *Kazuo Ohno's World: From Without and Within.* Wesleyan University Press, 2004. Translated by John Barrett.

Olivier Mythodrama. *Preparing Better Leaders.* Archetypes at Work Programme Handout, 2017.

Olivier Mythodrama. *Inspirational Leadership: Leadership Lessons from Henry V.* Course Outline, 2022. https://www.oliviermythodrama.com/ classic-programmes/inspirational-leadership/.

Olivier, Richard. *Shadow of the Stone Heart: A Search for Manhood.* Pan Books, 1995.

Pagel, Mark. *Wired for Culture: The Natural History of Human Cooperation.* Penguin, 2013.

Palmer, Parker. J. *Let Your Life Speak: Listening for the Voice of Vocation.* Jossey-Bass, 2024.

Pearlman, Steven. 'The Powerful Impact of the Theranos Whistleblower', *Forbes*, 13 December 2021. https://www.forbes.com/sites/stevenpearlman/2021/12/10/ the-powerful-impact-of-the-theranos-whistleblower/.

Perry, Christopher, and Rupert Tower (eds.). *Jung's Shadow Concept: The Hidden Light and Darkness within Ourselves.* Routledge, 2023.

Petriglieri, Jennifer, and Gianpiero Petriglieri. 'The Talent Curse', *Harvard Business Review*, May–June 2017. https://hbr.org/2017/05/ the-talent-curse.

Petriglieri, Gianpiero, and Mark Stein. 'The Unwanted Self: Projective Identification in Leaders' Identity Work', *Organisation Studies*, 33(9), 2012. http://gpetriglieri.com/wp-content/uploads/2017/01/ OrgStudies12-Unwanted-Self.pdf.

Pfeffer, Jeffrey. *Power: Why Some People Have It—And Others Don't.* HarperCollins, 2010.

Phillips, Adam. *Unforbidden Pleasures.* Farrar, Strauss and Giroux, 2016.

Pollan, Michael. *How to Change Your Mind: What the New Science of Psychedelics Teaches Us About Consciousness, Dying, Addiction, Depression, and Transcendence*. Penguin, 2018.

Porges, Stephen W. 'Orienting in a Defensive World: Mammalian Modifications of Our Evolutionary Heritage', *Psychophysiology*, July 1995. https://onlinelibrary.wiley.com/doi/10.1111/j.1469-8986.1995.tb01213.x.

Price, Devon. *Unlearning Shame: How Rejecting Self-Blame Culture Gives Us Real Power*. Monoray, 2024.

Pullman, Philip. *Dæmon Voices: Essays on Storytelling*. David Fickling Books, 2017.

Purser, Ronald E. *McMindfulness: How Mindfulness Became the New Capitalist Spirituality*. Repeater Books, 2019.

Raworth, Kate. *Doughnut Economics: Seven Ways to Think Like a 21st-Century Economist*. Random House Business Books, 2017.

Reitz, Megan, and John Higgins. *Speak Out, Listen Up: How to Have Conversations That Matter*. Pearson Education, 2024, second edition.

Richo, David. *Shadow Dance: Liberating the Power and Creativity of Your Dark Side*. Shambhala, 2024, twenty-fifth anniversary edition.

Robin, Vicki, and Joe Dominguez. *Your Money or Your Life: 9 Steps to Transforming Your Relationship with Money and Achieving Financial Independence*. Penguin, 2018, second revised edition.

Rodenburg, Patsy. *Presence: How to use Positive Energy for Success*. Penguin, 2009.

Rohr, Richard. *Falling Upward: A Spirituality for the Two Halves of Life*. Jossey-Bass, 2013.

Ronson, Jon. *So You've Been Publicly Shamed*. Picador, 2016, updated edition.

Rosenberg, Marshall. *Nonviolent Communication: A Language of Life*. PuddleDancer Press, 2015, third edition.

Rudd, Richard. *Gene Keys: Unlocking the Higher Purpose Hidden in Your DNA*. Watkins Publishing, 2013.

Sapolsky, Robert M. *Behave: The Biology of Humans at Out Best and Worst*. Penguin, 2017.

Sapolsky, Robert M. *Determined: A Science of Life without Free Will.* Penguin, 2023.

Scharmer, C. Otto. *Theory U: Leading from the Future as it Emerges—The Social Technology of Presencing.* Berrett–Koehler, 2009.

Schwartz, Richard C. *No Bad Parts: Healing Trauma and Restoring Wholeness with the Internal Family Systems Model.* Sounds True, 2021.

Sengupta, Shiv. 'How the Light Gets In', *Dark Knight of the Soul*, 20 August 2024. https://shivsengupta.substack.com/p/how-the-light-gets-in.

Sennett, Richard. *The Culture of the New Capitalism.* Yale University Press, 2006.

Seth, Anil. *Being You: A New Science of Consciousness.* Faber & Faber, 2021.

Shaw, Julia. *Making Evil: The Science Behind Humanity's Dark Side.* Canongate, 2019.

Shawcross, Harriet. *Unspeakable: The Things We Cannot Say.* Canongate, 2020.

Shragai, Naomi. *The Man Who Mistook His Job for His Life: How to Thrive at Work by Leaving Your Emotional Baggage Behind.* WH Allen, 2021.

Solzhenitsyn, Aleksandr. *The Gulag Archipelago, Volume 1.* Harper Perennial, 2007.

Stein, Mark. 'The Lost Good Self: Why the Whistleblower is Hated and Stigmatized', *Organisation Studies*, 42(7), 2019.

Stephens-Davidowitz, Seth. *Everybody Lies: What the internet Can Tell Us About Who We Really Are.* Bloomsbury, 2018.

Stoichita, Victor I. *A Short History of the Shadow.* Reaktion Books, 1997.

Stolzoff, Simone. *The Good Enough Job: Reclaiming Life from Work.* Portfolio, 2023.

Storr, Will. *The Status Game: On Social Position and How We Use It.* William Collins, 2021.

Stout, Martha. *The Sociopath Next Door.* Broadway Books, 2005.

Taffler, Adam. 'The Art of Giving and Receiving', *Togetherness*, 2024. https://www.togetherness.com/art-of-giving-and-receiving.

Talaga, Tanya. *All Our Relations: Indigenous Trauma in the Shadow of Colonialism*. Scribe, 2020.

Tallis, Raymond. *The Black Mirror: Looking at Life through Death*. Yale University Press, 2015.

Tanizaki, Jun'ichirō. *In Praise of Shadows*. Vintage, 2001. Translated by Thomas J Harper & Edward G. Seidensticker.

Taylor, Charles. *Modern Social Imaginaries*. Duke University Press, 2004.

Turkle, Sherry. *Alone Together: Why We Expect More from Technology and Less from Each Other*. Basic Books, 2017, third edition.

Tzu, Lao. *Tao Te Ching: A Book About the Way and the Power of the Way*. Shambhala, 1998. Translated by Ursula K. Le Guin with J. P. Seaton.

Vaihinger, Hans. *The Philosophy of 'As If'*. Routledge, 2021.

van der Kolk, Bessel A. *The Body Keeps the Score: Brain, Mind, and Body in the Healing of Trauma*. Penguin, 2015.

von Franz, Marie-Louise. *Creation Myths*. Shambhala, 2017, revised edition.

von Franz, Marie-Louise. *Shadow and Evil in Fairy Tales*. Shambhala, 2017, revised edition.

Vox Intra. *Shadow Seeker Card Deck: Exercises to Explore Your Subconscious and Embrace Your Dark Side*. Vox Intra, 2024.

Walsh, Mark. *Embodiment: Moving Beyond Mindfulness*. Unicorn Slayer Press, 2020.

Welwood, John. 'On Spiritual Bypassing and Relationship', *Science & Nonduality*, 10 February 2024. https://scienceandnonduality.com/article/on-spiritual-bypassing-and-relationship/.

West, Tessa. *Jerks at Work: Toxic Coworkers and What to Do About Them*. Ebury Edge, 2022.

Western, Simon. *Eco-Mutualism: Re-imagining Humanitarianism*. The Eco-Leadership Institute & Humanitarian Leadership Academy, 2024. https://www.humanitarianleadershipacademy.org/wp-content/uploads/2024/09/Eco-MutualismRe-imaginingHumanitarianismebook.pdf.

Western, Simon. 'The Politics of Dissonance: Harmony or Disharmony?', *Re-enchanting Our Worlds*, 12 August 2024. https://simonwestern.substack.com/p/the-politics-of-dissonance.

Whyte, David. *Consolations: The Solace, Nourishment and Underlying Meaning of Everyday Words*. Canongate, 2019.

Whyte, David. *River Flow: New and Selected Poems*. Many Rivers Press, 2012, revised edition.

Wilson, Sarah. 'Bullshit versus Lying', *This is Precious*, 22 August 2024. https://sarahwilson.substack.com/p/bullshit-versus-lying.

Wolynn, Mark. *It Didn't Start with You: How Inherited Family Trauma Shaped Who We Are and How to End the Cycle*. Viking, 2016.

Wynn-Williams, Sarah. *Careless People A Story of Where I Used to Work: Power, Greed, Madness*. Macmillan, 2025.

Yurchak, Alexei. *Everything Was Forever, Until It Was No More: The Last Soviet Generation*. Princeton University Press, 2005.

Zimbardo, Philip. *The Lucifer Effect: Understanding How Good People Turn Evil*. Random House, 2007.

Žižek, Slavoj. *Enjoy Your Symptom! Jacques Lacan in Hollywood and Out*. Routledge, 1992.

Zuboff, Shoshana. *The Age of Surveillance Capitalism: The Fight for a Human Future at the New Frontier of Power*. Profile Books, 2019.

Zweig, Connie. *The Inner Work of Age: Shifting from Role to Soul*. Park Street Press, 2021.

Zweig, Connie, and Jeremiah Abrams (eds.). *Meeting the Shadow: The Hidden Power of the Dark Side of Human Nature*. TarcherPerigee, 2020.

FURTHER RESOURCES

Workshops and resources by Richard Olivier and Laurence Hillman on embodying Leadership Archetypes. www.archetypesatwork.com

The Centre of Applied Jungian Studies, dedicated to teaching Jungian Psychology as a practical and accessible tool for personal individuation, increased consciousness and the restoration of meaning. www.appliedjung.com

The writings and workshops of the philosopher Bayo Alomolafe, who is also the founder of The Emergence Network. www.bayoakomolafe.net

David Burkus is the author of *Best Teams Ever* and a range of books offering new perspectives on leadership and management. www.davidburkus.com

Men's groups and a range of courses including Shadow Work, Self Leadership and Relationship Mastery led by Connor Beaton. www.connorbeaton.com

The writing and work of Tomas Chamorro-Premuzic, including his TED Talks. www.drtomas.com

Eco-Leadership is a groundbreaking approach that aligns leadership practice with ecosystem principles, creating organisations that are more engaged, purposeful and adaptive in the face of urgent challenges. www.ecoleadershipinstitute.org

The Global Society for Good Leadership is an independent organisation dedicated to advancing leadership excellence and ensuring the integrity of business and society. www.leadershipsociety.world

Heresy Consulting Ltd is a leadership development consultancy that applies depth psychology to the practical problems of organisational life. www.heresyconsulting.com

The website of Rob Chesnut, with links to his book *Intentional Integrity* and availability for speaking engagements on ethics and business. www.intentionalintegrity.com

Workshops led by Jamie Catto, including sessions on Transforming Shadows, and access to free resources and live events. www.JamieCatto.com

The website for UK-based registered psychotherapists and counsellors. www.psychotherapy.org.uk

Workshops and training relating to the 'Wheel of Consent,' covering intimacy, circling and communication. www.togetherness.com

Cinematic poetry by Paula Lavric on a range of relevant human themes. https://youtube.com/@undinepoetry

ACKNOWLEDGEMENTS

This book took five years from idea to publication, not due to the length of the text, but the nature of the subject matter. It required time to compost and for my thinking to evolve.

First, I would like to thank Richard Martin, my fantastic editor, who took my often-incoherent ideas and helped make sense of them and bring them to life on the page. Without you, this book would have remained an idea.

Thank you to Henry Steadman for the design of the intriguing book cover, Jesse May Palmer for the wonderful illustrations throughout and Caroline Li for the book design work.

Thank you to my publisher Martin Liu for believing in this book and agreeing to publish it, even though the title is far from conventional. I would like to thank Aiyana Curtis and the LID Business Media editorial team for their guidance and support in making it happen.

I would also like to thank Tomas Chamorro-Premuzic for writing the foreword, and for his great articles and research challenging conventional management and leadership thinking.

Thank you to all those who read the manuscript and contributed testimonials to support the book: Dan Pink, Chip Conley,

Patrick Clarke, Andy Lopata, Anushia Reddy, David Burkus, Christian Busch, Stuart Crainer, Jennifer Petriglieri, Michael Bungay Stanier, Shakil Nathoo, James Woodcock, Laurence Barrett, Joseph Pistrui, Santiago Iniguez de Onzono, Mark Wright, Megan Reitz, Adam Taffler, Simon Western, Marshall Goldsmith, Otti Vogt, Nina Kreyer, Gulammabas Lakha, Itay Talgam, Michael Frawley, Samir Rath, Tim Lebrecht, Perry Timms, and Jamie Catto.

This book would not have been possible without the contributions of the many people who generously shared their insights and were interviewed for it. I could not include every idea or story but sincerely thank everybody who contributed or assisted in any way. If I have omitted anyone, the failure is totally mine, and I thank you, too, for your support.

I would like to thank:

Aayush Surana, Chris Adler, Alina Costache, Doshin Nelson Roshi, Iulia Mazilu, Paul McNicholl, Bayo Akomolafe, Kenny Mammarella-D'Cruz, Peter Tyler, Nick Filloy, Joseph Pistrui, Shiv Sengupta, Francis Briers, Jojo Fresnedi, Robert Chesnut, Richard Olivier, Khuyen Bui, Neil Gibb, and Phil Birkin.

Thank you to my colleagues at Korn Ferry for providing a stimulating working environment to learn and grow in.

Thank you to Dominika for encouraging me to keep going and not give up; your support was invaluable.

Thank you to my family and my close friends, all of whom often witness the worst of my Shadow side and love me still.

Finally, I'd like to thank you, dear reader, for being willing to read this book and to face your own Shadows.

ABOUT THE AUTHOR

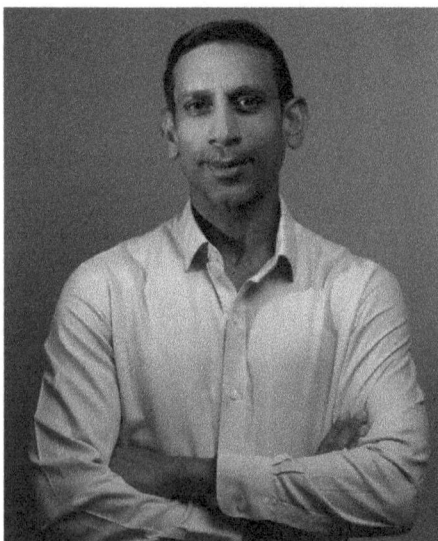

Steven D'Souza is a Senior Client Partner at Korn Ferry's Leadership and Professional Development Practice. He is an educator, executive coach and keynote speaker. He has authored or co-authored six books: *Made in Britain, Brilliant Networking, Not Knowing, Not Doing, Not Being* and *Shadows at Work*. Steven has been recognised by Thinkers50 on its RADAR list and included in *HR Magazine's* Most Influential list. His work has been featured in UK and international media, including *Harvard Business Review, Bloomberg, The Independent, The Guardian* and *The Sunday Times*. Steven is passionate about helping leaders explore purpose and meaning in their lives, make transitions in their careers and find fulfilment. His work blends contemplative wisdom, spirituality, psychology and philosophy with practical approaches to career, leadership and organisational development.

He can be contacted at **stevendsouza.com** for keynotes, workshops, consulting and coaching.